5 Ways To Get A Raise

Greater Influence = Greater Income

Written By
John Barrett

Published by
Rocket Publishing

Copyright © 2019 John Barrett
All rights reserved.
ISBN: 0-9888284-8-0
ISBN-13: 978-0-9888284-8-3

Published By: Rocket Publishing

Book Design By: John Barrett Art
www.johnbarrettart.com

Thanks:

My amazing wife, Erin, our two beautiful girls, Zion & Allie, and our little man, Isaiah. They teach me more about leadership than anyone else ever could. To everyone who helped bring this book together with their appreciated input. To my mentor Dr. John C. Maxwell for showing me the way.

CONTENT:

Intro —————————————————— 7

#1 > Honor Those Above You ——————— 13
   Speak Highly ————————————— 17
   Soak Up ——————————————— 25
   S.E.R.V.E. —————————————— 33

#2 > Do More Than Expected ——————— 41
   Make It Better ————————————— 45
   Make It Bigger ————————————— 53
   Make It Brighter ———————————— 59

#3 > Exploit Your Strengths ——————— 67
   Know Your Strengths ——————————— 73
   Grow Your Strengths ———————————— 79
   Show Your Strengths ———————————— 87

#4 > Run Up The Score ———————————— 93
   Who ————————————————— 97
   What ————————————————— 103
   When ————————————————— 109
   Where ———————————————— 115
   Why ————————————————— 121

#5 > Lead Yourself —————————————— 127
   Remember ————————————————— 131
   Resolve ——————————————————— 139
   Retreat ——————————————————— 149

Conclusion ————————————————— 159

Intro

You deserve a raise.

At least you will if you follow the principles laid out in this book. But first, you must understand that a raise doesn't have anything to do with money. Did you get that? Let me say it again for dramatic effect…a raise doesn't have anything to do with money. Financial compensation is merely a byproduct of the value you add. The more influential you are, the more valuable you'll become. The formula is actually quite simple:

$$I + I = I$$

Influence plus (more) Influence equals Income. And the more I's (Influence) you add to the equation the greater your income will be. Here is the infinity formula you could carry on forever:

$$I + I + I + I + I + I + I + I + I + I + I + I + I + I + I + I = Ix$$

Consistently increase your influence, and watch your income soar.

I have coached many people, from entry-level employees to high-profile CEOs, and the common denominator they all share is their capacity and commitment to raising their influence. You, too, are created with the ability to go as far as your dedication will take you. You possess unlimited potential to be, do, and have more. Success is an equal opportunity outcome if you are willing to put forth the effort. It isn't reserved for some and withheld from others.

Life is like a bank account: what you deposit into it is what you'll withdraw from it. Your value is only limited by the cap you put on it. And the only person responsible for raising your value is…you! If you don't value yourself, don't expect others to value you either. If you don't expect greatness to come out of you, don't expect others to see the greatness in you. If you want to get better at what you do, you have to get better at who you are. Always remember that leadership is the inward work which leads to outward behavior.

When you conquer yourself, you can attain your dreams. You'll come to a place where you have overthrown your feelings of fear, worthlessness, failure, pride, worry, and your self-limiting beliefs. The best leaders possess confidence in who they are and what they can accomplish. It's not a matter of ego, but healthy self-assurance. Philosopher Lao Tzu said, "He who conquers men is strong; he who conquers himself is mighty." When you exterminate the enemy within, you liberate the warrior inside. If you want to lead the masses, you have to first start by leading yourself. Leading yourself is about exterminating the damaging beliefs which limit your ability to influence others.

Influence is the currency of leadership. You determine your income by how much you invest in learning how to influence others, followed by acting on that knowledge. When your influence goes to the next level, you'll raise your value to the company and those around you. Influencers receive greater compensation because of what they bring to the table. In 1921, Charles Schwab was one of the first American businessmen to be paid over a million-dollar salary by U.S. Steel owner Andrew Carnegie. What's interesting is that Schwab didn't know much at all about steel or manufacturing. However, here is what he said about why he was paid so well: "I consider my ability to arouse enthusiasm among my people the greatest asset I possess, and the way to develop the best that is in a person is by appreciation and encouragement." Schwab became incredibly wealthy by becoming a great influencer.

Is it all about the money? Of course not. But as Zig Ziglar always said, "Money won't make you happy, but everybody wants to find out for themselves." Building wealth opens up the door for more opportunities to provide for yourself, your family, your charities, and to have a greater impact on the world. As you level up your leadership ability, you'll increase your capacity to make more money. Intentional learners are exceptional earners.

A Columbia University study by Melinda Tamkins showed that success in the workplace is guaranteed not by what or whom you know, but ultimately by your popularity. In her research, Tamkins found that "Popular workers were seen as trustworthy, motivated, serious, decisive and hardworking and were recommended for fast-track promotion and generous pay increases. Their less-liked colleagues were perceived as arrogant, conniving and manipulative. Pay raises and promotions were ruled out regardless of their academic background or professional qualifications." Being popular is not reserved for charismatic personalities or extroverts; it's reserved for anyone who makes a significant difference through their efforts.

Influence is your ticket to the top. The more you learn the art of how to make a positive impact on other people, the more you'll advance. The strategies I lay out in this book will give you a game plan for becoming the person of influence you dream of becoming. It's your choice whether or not to follow them. You can either remain as you are and never advance in life or work, or you can follow them, and they will guide you to new levels of influence, and open up the door for greater income.

Get ready to discover the five ways to get a raise!

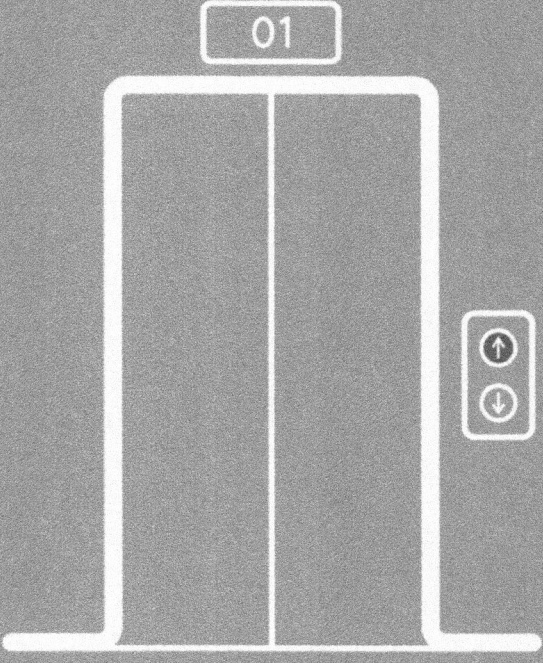

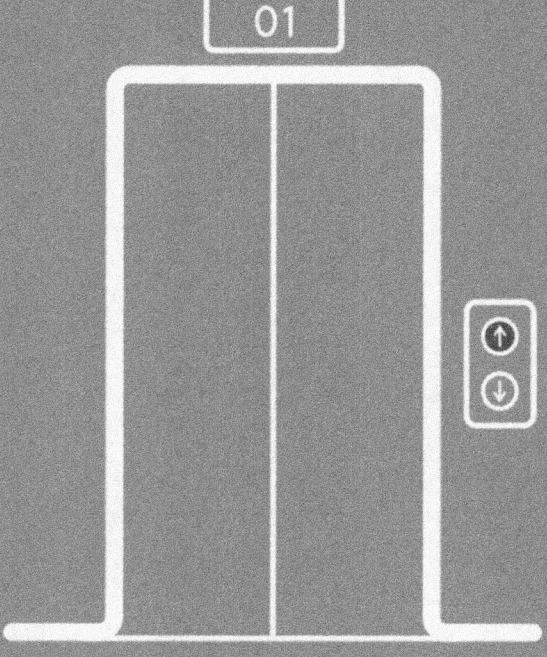

1

Way #1
Honor Those Above You

The concept of honor has all but been erased from my generation and those that have come after. Honoring those in authority over us has become confused with earning respect. Honor is not dependent on performance or likability; it is something due to every person based on their intrinsic worth as human beings. Choosing to honor those around you will have a reciprocal effect. Nothing raises your level of influence more than showing honor to those in authority over you.

When you honor—and show respect to—your superiors, you will gain their trust. Trust is the currency of leaders; it is their relational bank account. The more they sense that you honor them, the more trust they will invest in you. Your honor establishes what I like to call a "Trust Fund." This fund determines your level of influence. Honor given is trust received, and your trust fund increases with each deposit. However, the opposite is also true: if you fail to honor your leaders, you will bankrupt your "trust fund" and lose your influence.

Have you ever considered the possibility of leading your superiors? When those in authority trust you, they will seek your insight into matters, and you can impact the decisions they make.

Have you ever noticed how some people seem to have the ear of their leaders, while others can barely garner a "hello"? Which one are you? Which one would you like to be?

The more you develop your ability to honor those above you, the more influence you can potentially have on your whole organization. I'm not talking about ingratiating yourself. Neither does it involve lying, cheating, or manipulating your leaders. Honor must be genuine to be sustainable and influential. Author Darren Hardy wrote, "When people fake anything, they only produce more fakeness, and that leads to disconnect, trouble, misery and ultimately failure."

Honor must come from a genuine alignment of what you say and do.

Here are three tips to help you truly honor those in authority over you: speak highly of them, soak in much, and S.E.R.V.E. continuously.

HONOR THOSE ABOVE YOU

SPEAK HIGHLY

1.1

SPEAK HIGHLY

The way you talk about your superiors will become a self-fulfilling prophecy; how you talk about them is the way they will talk about you someday. You cannot show honor to those in authority if you are bad-mouthing them. Words are like boomerangs: whatever you release will return even faster. The way you speak will either assist or resist your success.

"Words are like boomerangs: whatever you release will return even faster."

Your lack of support will stunt your level of influence. No matter how secretive you think you are in your conversations, your negative views will always be revealed. Words are powerful; they cannot be contained, and they always evoke a response, whether good, bad, or indifferent. What you say will find its way. Words are constantly at work affecting outcomes, and their impact can carry momentum long after they are first spoken.

Author Napoleon Hill said, "Think twice before you speak, because your words and influence will plant the seed of either success or failure in the mind of another." Words are like seeds that will eventually produce sweet fruits or bitter roots. We must be careful and intentional about the words we communicate, especially when it comes to how we speak about those in authority over us. Author Mireille Guiliano said, "Intelligence, knowledge, or experience are important and might get you a job, but strong communication skills are what will get you promoted."

When communicating with your leaders, here are three things to consider:

BUILD ON THEIR IDEAS

Many people come out of the gate swinging, tearing down everyone else's ideas so theirs win. The moment you start attacking other people's ideas is the moment you ring the fight bell. No one likes to have their ideas shot down. Instead, build on your leaders' ideas. Instead of criticizing their point of view, or striving to get your own point across, acknowledge their idea and identify a positive aspect of it. Find something you can build upon, rather than dismantling it.

Remove "can't" from your vocabulary. Instead of saying, "It can't be done," focus on how to make the idea work. Being a negative Nelly will only lead to your own demise. Spend more time wow-ing ideas to life than how-ing them to death. You certainly have the right to disagree with the ideas and decisions your leaders make, but do not be contentious about it. At the end of the day, you have to either get on board or jump ship…just don't cause a mutiny. Control your tongue, and you'll control your future.

Ask questions to gain clarity. Perhaps there was something you missed. Even if you disagree with an idea, don't start there. Start by asking questions and seeking to understand the problem someone is trying to solve. Every idea is ultimately an attempt to address an issue, concern, or opportunity. Get to the heart of the idea in order to influence a different outcome. Define the problem to determine the best solution. In his book, Making Collaboration Work, David Strauss said, "If you can't agree on the problem, you won't agree on the solution."

Build on each other's ideas rather than tearing them down, and you'll come up with a collaborative solution in the end.

Spend more time wow-ing ideas to life than you do how-ing them to death.

STAY GENUINELY POSITIVE

I love to play Scrabble. Of course, the point of the game is to strategically place your words to get the highest point value based on the tiles used. The way you use your words determines how high you score, which determines whether you win or lose. Life works much like Scrabble; how we use our words will determine our outcome.

The way in which you talk about situations gives others a quick judgment about you. How you communicate sets the tone for your reputation. You must hold yourself to a higher standard than others hold you to. Even if you are right, it does not give you the right to get upset at everyone else who doesn't see it yet. Your influence will diminish the moment you start to get frustrated with your leaders. Remember, you are there to work for and with others, not to trample over them. So watch your attitude and make sure you are not letting your impatience get the best of you.

Toxic words create toxic outcomes. No one wants to be around a complainer who is always talking negatively about everything and everyone. Leaders have little tolerance for destructive words. The truth is, you attract what you talk about. When you speak negatively, you will draw more negativity. Misery loves company. Success also loves company and draws people to it. What goes around comes around. Be a hope-giver in your organization and influence others with your genuine optimism.

> "You must hold yourself to a higher standard than others hold you to."

We must protect our words with the utmost care and intention, knowing that they will determine our future. Guarding our lips means we have to be mindful and strategic about the words we use and the words we allow to come out of our mouth.

SPEAK THEIR LANGUAGE

Every leader has a unique dialect by which they communicate their ideas and expectations. In order to successfully interact with and convey your ideas to them, you must adopt their terminology, and not expect them to adapt to yours.

If you traveled to another country that didn't speak your native language, you would certainly attempt to learn some of their language beforehand in order to navigate the area and make basic conversation. The same is true when dealing with those in leadership. Figure out their language and begin speaking it. The more common ground you establish with your leaders, the quicker they will identify you as someone worth investing time and money in. If you only focus on what you are passionate about, at the expense of understanding others' ideas, you will alienate the very people you are trying to reach.

Listen first, speak later. Speaking rashly allows the tyranny of the moment to dictate what we say. We speak from a place of jealousy, pride, or fear. We do not listen with the intent to understand others and find common ground with them. The goal here is to guard our words. People who do not guard their mouths lack power because they lack self-control. Take your time, and choose your words wisely. It will save you a lot of regret and back-tracking to fix the damage you have caused with your brash responses.

When you listen, you learn how to speak in your leaders' language, and when you respond in kind, you will make a stronger connection with them. If you want to be a person of influence among your leaders, be supportive of them and look for ways to make their ideas come to life. Discover their distinctive dialects and identify their fundamental values. Adopt them as your own and watch your influence grow.

REVIEW
5 WAYS TO GET A RAISE
#1 — HONOR THOSE ABOVE YOU

(1.1) Speak Highly
    a) Build On Their Ideas
    b) Stay Genuinely Positive
    c) Speak Their Language

HONOR THOSE ABOVE YOU

SOAK UP MUCH

Soak Up Much

Great leaders are like sponges; they soak up as much as they can from their leaders.

Early in my leadership journey, I was fortunate to be surrounded by leaders who poured into my life, but I learned it was up to me to be available for what they had to offer. I remember a critical meeting held by the organization I was with at the time. Attendance was mandatory that day, but the timing didn't fit into my already overloaded schedule, which was filled with other meetings and preparations for a large event.

Reluctantly, I slipped away from my event planning duties to attend the company meeting. I spent the entire time sneaking glances at my watch and thinking about my other responsibilities, anxious to get back to what I had been doing before.

Finally, the meeting ended, and I darted out the back door after saying my goodbyes and quickly shaking hands. As I strode down the hallway, the leader of the organization, who had facilitated the meeting, caught up with me and put his arm around my shoulder.

He smiled at me and said, "John, I know you are busy and working very hard right now, but I want you to know that when you come to a meeting, I want your mind and heart present. I saw you watching your clock and keeping your head down, disengaged. These meetings are vital to our company moving forward, and you are an example to everyone else in that room. I need you alert next time because you have too much to offer." Dan could have just corrected me and moved on, but he continued by taking the time to identify the strengths and talents he saw in me and to affirm the positive impact I was having on the organization. "Keep up the good work!" he encouraged as we parted ways.

I will never forget that moment. At first, I was embarrassed. Then, I started to mentally defend myself, saying that he didn't know how busy I really was. But, as he continued, I realized he was right to call me out. From that day on, I decided that, wherever I am, I will do all I can to be fully present in the moment. Because Dan took the time to both correct and encourage me, and I was able to open myself up to receive his correction, I became a better leader moving forward.

We need to receive correction and instruction from our leaders humbly. If your superiors consistently feel frustrated that you do not listen to them, you will lose opportunities from them. By remaining attentive to them, you can pick up great tips from your leaders on a regular basis, both by watching what they do and listening to what they say. Not only can you learn what to do, but you can also learn what not to do; both will accelerate your success tremendously. Be committed to learning and growth as you serve under leadership.

> "If your superiors consistently feel frustrated that you do not listen to them, you will lose opportunities from them."

If a person can't be led they aren't fit to lead. The more you learn from them, the more you can earn from them.

Two ways to develop a sponge-like character when soaking up the lessons your leaders have to offer are: humility and hunger.

HUMILITY

John Wooden said, "It's what you learn after you know it all that counts."

We all know one: the "Couch Coach." They sit on the couch eating potato chips while yelling out every call the coach should have made in the game they're watching on TV. Convinced they know it all and wondering why it isn't them calling the shots on the sidelines, they fail to see how their own calls don't always work out.

Just like a "couch coach," we can fall prey to the same pitfall: thinking that we already know it all and have nothing to learn from others. However, the more we think we know, the less we try to learn. Humility is the key which unlocks knowledge and creativity. Without it, we become stagnant and unproductive in our thinking. Only when we admit that we don't know it all are we able to open the door to unlimited possibilities.

At age 94, Pablo Casals was considered one of the greatest cellists of all time. After one of his last concerts at the Kennedy Center in Washington D.C., someone asked him why he still practiced over three hours a day. He responded, "I think I am making progress. To retire is the beginning of death." Be humble enough to admit you always have more to learn.

HUNGER

It is said that a proud young man once approached Socrates seeking wisdom. He walked up to him and said, "O great Socrates, I come to you for wisdom."

Socrates, recognizing a pompous fool when he saw one, led him down to the sea and took him chest deep into the water. Then he asked him, "What did you say you wanted?"
"Wisdom, O great Socrates," said the young man.
Socrates put his hands on the man's shoulders and pushed him under. Thirty seconds later Socrates let him up. "What do you want?" he asked again.
"Wisdom," the young man sputtered, "O great and wise Socrates."
Socrates pushed him under again. Thirty seconds, thirty-five, forty–then Socrates let him up. The man was gasping. "What do you want, young man?"
Between heavy breaths, the man wheezed, "Wisdom! O wise and wonderful…"
Socrates jammed him under again–forty seconds passed, and then fifty–then he let him up. "What do you want?"
"Air!" the young man yelled. "I need air!" Socrates replied, "When you want wisdom as much as you have just wanted air, then you will begin to find wisdom."

In order to be successful, you must have an insatiable hunger for learning and self-improvement. In fact, if you study the most successful people throughout history, the one common denominator is their commitment to self-improvement. There is an old saying: "When the student is ready the teacher will appear." If you become a willing student, you will find there are teachers all around, showing you the way. By remaining in a growth mindset and challenging yourself every day to get better and never settle, you will position yourself for continued success throughout life.

If you want to be successful, you have to have an insatiable desire to learn and get better.

REVIEW
5 WAYS TO GET A RAISE
#1 — HONOR THOSE ABOVE YOU

(1.1) Speak Highly
    a) Build On Their Ideas
    b) Stay Genuinely Positive
    c) Speak Their Language

(1.2) Soak Up Much
    a) Humility
    b) Hunger

HONOR THOSE ABOVE YOU

S.E.R.V.E.

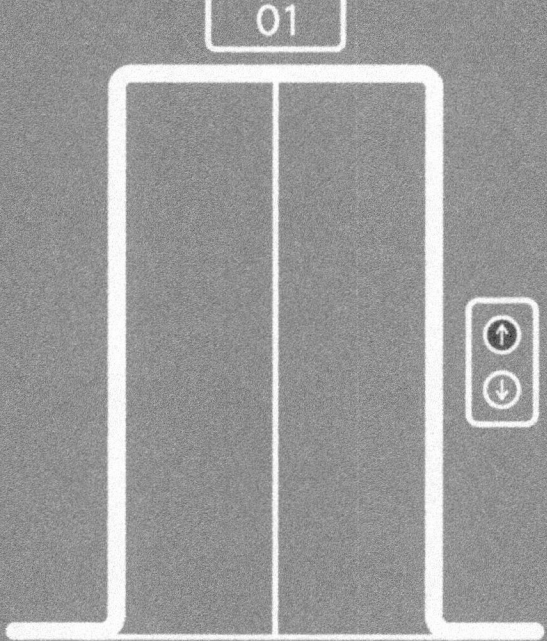

S.E.R.V.E.

If you can't S.E.R.V.E., you can't lead

When you lift your leaders up, you'll rise with them. Some of the most successful people throughout history rose through the ranks by serving someone who brought them up the mountaintop of success. No one starts out at the top; it is only because of their willingness to work hard and serve others that they were able to elevate their position. Some of the greatest leaders began as humble followers; by serving those above them, they achieved a higher level of success for themselves. Merle Crowell, an American author who spent a great deal of time with John D. Rockefeller, Jr. and many other successful leaders said, "It is the men behind who make the man ahead."

Robert Greenleaf, the founder of the modern servant leadership movement and the Greenleaf Center for Servant Leadership, said, "Good leaders must first become good servants." If you think serving is below you, then leadership is beyond you. Those who are willing to serve are the ones who are eligible to truly succeed. When you change your mindset from "What can I get?" to "What can I give?" you will become more and more valuable to those around you.

Humility is a word we don't typically emphasize in the business world, but its effect is monumental. We tend to think success is characterized by fearlessness, boldness, and strength. We associate humility with weakness, when it's the humble who truly possess the most power. Serving others takes a great measure of confidence and boldness. Artist and poet Kahlil Gibran said, "Tenderness and kindness are not signs of weakness and despair, but manifestations of strength and resolution."

Humility is strong, bold, and fearless. It takes much more strength to walk in humility than it does to stand out in pride. Ego is one of the greatest limiters of influence. e Author Gordon MacDonald said, "You can tell whether you are becoming a servant by how you act when you're treated like one." Serving others is not just about what we do, it's about who we are. Make it a point to serve someone every day and your influence will grow stronger because of it.

Here is a great acronym that will help you remember to S.E.R.V.E.

S=SIMPLE

Serving doesn't have to be complicated or elaborate. Don't make it hard to be a servant. Don't wait to do everything before you do something. If you wait to do something until you can do everything, you won't do anything. Just start with what you can do. It's not always the big things that make the biggest difference; sometimes, the smallest gestures make the greatest impact. I have heard that tiny termites do more physical damage in a year's time

> "If you wait to do something until you can do everything, you won't do anything."

than all natural disasters combined. Small acts of kindness and service go a long way. The important thing is to be sincere about whatever you decide to do. President Theodore Roosevelt said, "No one cares how much you know until they know how much you care." Make it a point to serve someone today.

E=Enthusiastic

Nothing is worse than someone who is helping with a bad attitude. If you're going to serve others, be excited about the opportunity and consider it a privilege to serve them. Don't walk around with a frown on your face, complaining about what you "have to do" for others. Identify your purpose in serving and focus on that. Be grateful for the opportunity to be able to help others. Your eagerness to serve makes others feel valuable. No one wants to feel like a burden. Serving is a privilege, not a burden; don't ever confuse the two.

R=Random

Service doesn't always need an intricately designed plan. Serving spontaneously can be equally effective—and fun! If you see a need, step out and meet it. Serve others when they least expect it; what a lovely surprise to give. Think about how much it has meant to you when someone has dropped whatever they were doing to help you with an unexpected need. Pay it forward. Spontaneous, random, genuine help impacts people's lives, not just in the moment but for a long time after. The less they expect it, the greater the impact it will make. Be willing to put others ahead of your agenda, and you'll have influence everywhere you go. Random acts of kindness result in specific acts of gratitude.

V=Voluntary

Don't wait to be asked to serve; be someone who takes the initiative. Serve without expecting anything in return. The word "volunteer" is defined as a person who does some act or enters into a transaction without being under any legal obligation to do so, and without being promised any remuneration for his services. Volunteers serve from the heart. John Bunyan said, "You have not lived today unless you've done something for someone who can never repay you."

If you are forced to serve someone or are doing it because you "have to," it loses its meaning. People are impacted by those that do something for them without feeling coerced or guilted into it. A significant connection takes place when people feel they are worth your time and effort.

E=Enduring

Keep on serving. I have met many leaders who felt they had "paid their dues" and no longer needed to serve. They thought they had somehow graduated from a life of service. But, serving is a life-long endeavor. It is a lifestyle of valuing people. No matter how successful you get, you are always called to serve others.

> "The payoff from serving far outweighs the comfort of sitting."

Don't grow weary from serving. It is hard work and will require blood, sweat, and even tears at times. Don't stop because of the effort it takes. The payoff from serving far outweighs the comfort of sitting. It takes humility to surrender your selfishness and energy. Do take care to pace yourself (to avoid burnout) and to guard yourself against those who "use" you, but it's always better to err on the side of service rather than selfishness. Arthur Ashe said, "True heroism is remarkably sober, very undramatic, not the urge to surpass all others at whatever the cost but the urge to serve others whatever the cost."

REVIEW
5 WAYS TO GET A RAISE
#1 — HONOR THOSE ABOVE YOU

(1.1) Speak Highly
    a) Build On Their Ideas
    b) Stay Genuinely Positive
    c) Speak Their Language

(1.2) Soak Up Much
    a) Humility
    b) Hunger

(1.3) S.E.R.V.E.
    a) S=Simple
    b) E=Enthusiastic
    c) R=Random
    d) V=Voluntary
    e) E=Enduring

Way #2
Do More Than Expected

Actions speak louder than words ever will. It is not what someone claims they can do but what they actually do that makes a difference. Great leaders don't make excuses; they capitalize on opportunities. It's their discipline to action which sets them apart from everyone else.

I heard a great story about a shoe manufacturing plant that sent a representative to Africa to sell shoes. Upon his arrival in Africa, he realized that everyone was barefooted. Returning home, he said, "It's no use. No one there wears shoes." Later, the company sent another man to Africa. Shortly after his arrival, he wrote back, "What a wonderful market! Everyone here needs shoes!"

The difference between successful people and unsuccessful people lies not in what they know, but in what they are willing to do. What sets high achievers apart from everyone else is their defining courage which enables them to abandon excuses, take risks, and move toward results. Successful

> "The difference between successful people and unsuccessful people lies not in what they know, but in what they are willing to do."

people see opportunities where others only see obstacles. They see the potential of what could be instead of complaining about what isn't. Coach Wooden put it this way, "Do not let what you cannot do interfere with what you can do." Indecision to action kills opportunity.

If you want to raise your influence, become a doer. There is a big difference between what I call doers and don'ters.

- Doers are people of action: they see the possibilities and make things happen
- Don'ters are people of excuses: they always have a reason for why things didn't happen.

President Calvin Coolidge said, "Nothing in the world can take the place of persistence. Talent will not; nothing is more common than unsuccessful men with talent. Genius will not; unrewarded genius is almost a proverb. Education will not; the world is full of educated derelicts. Persistence and determination are omnipotent."

Don'ters are whiners, not winners. They continually gripe about the amount of effort it takes to get something done. Don'ters do not thrive; they live in survival mode. They consistently choose the path of least resistance and expend the least amount of energy. Don'ters look at a situation and find all the ways it won't work out, and then replay those negative messages over and over again in their minds. They get stuck in paralysis of analysis and rarely step out to do more than what little is expected of them.

Doers, on the other hand, are in it to win it. They simply can't settle for average. They are willing and determined to put in the hours and energy necessary to succeed. In fact, doers put in extra work, causing something ordinary to become extraordinary. They think through every possible scenario, strategizing ways to make things excellent. Doers are leaders. They do more than expected, causing them to deliver more than expected. Zig Ziglar said, "When you do more than you get paid for eventually you'll be paid for more than you do."

Here are three ways to do more than what is expected:

2.1

MAKE IT BETTER

The real question you need to ask yourself about your job is, "Is this company better because I am part of it?" The mark of a great leader is their ability to add value. They enhance the quality of whatever they touch. They are constantly thinking about ways to improve those things they are a part of. Author Marcus Buckingham wrote, "'I am not satisfied' is the mantra of a leader. As a leader, you are never satisfied with the present, because in your head you can see a better future, and the friction between the 'what is' and the 'what could be' burns you, stirs you, and propels you forward. This is leadership."

If you want to do more than what is expected of you, always seek out better and more efficient ways of operating. Improve upon your ideas and the ideas of those around you. The results you are currently getting are a direct outcome of the way you are thinking about and doing things. To improve your results, you have to change what you are doing. As the saying goes, "You can't get what you've never got until you do something you've never done."

> "You can't get what you've never got until you do something you've never done."

High achievers are willing to think at a higher level than anyone else around them. Albert Einstein said, "We cannot solve our problems with the same thinking we used when we created them." In order to move beyond our current level, we have to rise up to a new level of thinking. This requires a willingness to spend time working on your business, not just in it. Very few take the time to develop better practices because they are inundated with the daily to do's. They spend more time putting out fires rather than lighting new ones.

If you want to raise your level of influence, make things better around you.

Here are three ways you can do so:

Pursue Excellence

If you want to be the best, you have to get around the best. Surround yourself with opportunities which will help spark new ideas. Ed Catmull, the President of Pixar and Walt Disney Animation Studios, shares many stories in his book Creativity Inc. about how committed they were to pursuing excellence while developing their movies. He tells about the trips they would send their creative team on to help them become fully submerged in the experience of an upcoming film. For example, while working on the famous movie Ratatouille, they sent their team to Paris to visit fine dining restaurants and tour their kitchens and to walk around the city's sewers to fully immerse themselves in a rat's life. While working on Finding Nemo, their team trained to get scuba certifications. There is a reason why Pixar is the best at producing animated films; it isn't a mere coincidence, it's their commitment to excellence.

In order to improve upon that which you are working on, you have to improve your upon that which you are surrounded by. If you want to make things better, you have to immerse yourself in environments and experiences that will give you greater ideas than you currently have. Seek out anything that will fill you with new ideas and vision for the future. Eleanor Roosevelt said, "Small minds discuss people; average minds discuss events; great minds discuss ideas." Pursue excellence in all that you do, and all that you do will get better and better.

PROVIDE SOLUTIONS

To make things better, you have to become a great problem solver. Your influence grows as you provide solutions to problems. All business transactions are the result of someone paying to get a problem solved, whether meaningful or minuscule. The more you are able to provide solutions for people's problems, the more valuable you become to them. This ability requires that you bring unique ideas to the table. You can't just be a thermometer; you have to become a thermostat.

> "The more you are able to provide solutions for people's problems, the more valuable you become to them."

Thermometers read the temperature, but thermostats are able to change the temperature. Don't just bring problems to the table… offer solutions for them. No one wants to pay to find out they have a problem, but they will pay exceptionally well to get a problem fixed. Make it your practice never to bring a problem without a solution for it. Presenting a problem without a solution is really just a complaint in camouflage.

If you are struggling to find a solution, keep searching until you find one. Businessman J.P. Morgan said, "No problem can be solved until it is reduced to some simple form. The changing of a vague difficulty into a specific, concrete form is a very essential element in thinking." Don't give up on finding solutions; you may be moments away from a big breakthrough. Albert Einstein used to say, "It's not that I'm so smart, it's just that I stay with problems longer." It was his tenacity that enabled him to outlast his problems.

PERSIST RELENTLESSLY

Thomas Edison said, "When you have exhausted all possibilities, remember this–you haven't." The only way you truly lose is to give up. Sounds simple, but the truth is nothing is impossible until you give up. Successful people are those who don't give up.

We all face obstacles on our journey to success. We all encounter resistance. The only way to be successful is to develop what I call "persistence in resistance." You have to fight through the forces holding you back. Resistance is, in fact, one of the best teachers in our pursuit of success. Henry Ford said, "When everything seems to be going against you, remember that the airplane takes off against the wind, not with it." If you can harness resistance, you can rise above it.

Many people who face obstacles become disillusioned, thinking something is wrong. Obstacles are not always a sign of things going wrong. The path of success is not all smooth seas and warm breezes. Be patient and persistent. Change does not come overnight. Over time, you will work through your challenges. Remember, those with the greatest stamina will finish the race.

Develop an unwavering sense of determination, so that you don't give up when things get shaky…and things always get shaky. Radio personality Paul Harvey used to say, "You can tell you're on the road to success; it's uphill all the way."

The only way you truly lose is to give up.

REVIEW
5 WAYS TO GET A RAISE
#2 — DO MORE THAN EXPECTED

(2.1) Make It Better
    a) Pursue Excellence
    b) Provide Solutions
    c) Persist Relentlessly

2.2

MAKE IT BIGGER

You can tell if someone is a leader by how they treat the projects assigned to them. Successful people take what is given to them and add value to it. Unsuccessful people take what is given to them and diminish it. They try to minimize tasks, so they don't have to put in any substantial effort. The real test of successful leaders is to see what they do with what is given to them. Great leaders make things happen, average leaders watch things happen, and bad leaders ask, "What just happened?"

Healthy things grow. The healthier your leaders are, the faster your organization grows. However, unhealthy things (and people) begin to decay and waste away. The hard question you have to ask yourself is: "Am I helping us to grow as a result of my leadership?" Walt Disney said, "We keep moving forward, opening new doors, and doing new things, because we're curious and curiosity keeps leading us down new paths." He understood that great leadership always seeks to advance. My mentor, Dr. John C. Maxwell, shared the following story in his book, Sometimes You Win, Sometimes You Learn…

There's a story of a salesman from the eastern United States who arrived at a frontier town somewhere in the Old West. As the salesman was talking with the owner of the general store a rancher came in. The owner excused himself to take care of the customer. The rancher gave the storekeeper a list of things he needed, but he wanted credit to purchase them.

"Are you doing any fencing this spring?" asked the storekeeper.

"Sure am," said the rancher.

"Fencing in or fencing out?"

"Fencing in. Taking in another 360 acres across the creek."

"Good to hear it, Josh. You got credit. Just tell Harry out back what you need."

The salesman was confused. "I've seen all kinds of credit systems," he said, "but never one like that. How does it work?"

"Well," said the storekeeper, "if a man's fencing out, that means he's on the defensive, just trying to keep what he's got. But if he's fencing in, he's growing and getting bigger. I always give credit to a man who's fencing in, because that means he's got hope."

Here are three ways you can make things bigger:

PUSH YOUR LIMITS

T.S. Eliot said, "Only those who will risk going too far can possibly find out how far one can go." Only doing what you are comfortable with will never take you to greater heights. When you get to a point where you're in over your head, it doesn't really matter how much deeper you go. You're already in over your head, so dive deeper! Feeling overwhelmed by your potential and underwhelmed by your ability to succeed can either discourage you or drive you forward.

The issue lies in how you respond. If you let discouragement set in, you will give up your pursuit for more. But if you allow discipline to motivate you, it can drive you to pursue greater possibilities. Extraordinary leaders are willing to step out even when the task ahead seems insurmountable. They understand that true growth takes place outside of their comfort zone. The next level of success for you does not lie in what you have already accomplished; it waits outside your current level of accomplishment.

You will never be more than you are now unless you try something you've never done before. All great advancements were the result of someone attempting something that was beyond their comfort level. Exploring new ideas comes with a cost: abandoning your limiting fear. If your dreams don't scare you, you're not dreaming big enough. You'll become successful when your dreams are greater than your excuses.

> "You'll become successful when your dreams are greater than your excuses."

CREATIVELY COLLABORATE

Two horses can together pull about 9,000 lb. How much do you think four horses can pull? It would be reasonable to assume that four horses could pull 18,000 lb. However, four horses can actually pull over 30,000 lb. Collaboration doesn't double your effort; it multiplies your effort. There is a compound effect that occurs when creative collaboration takes place. If you truly want to multiply your impact, you must work with others. Going solo only limits your impact.

When you work alone, you have to work ten times as hard to produce something. Trying to be a creative Rambo and change the world by yourself is a set-up for disaster. In the real world, extraordinary accomplishments are the result of a team working together toward a common purpose. The better the team works together, the bigger the possibilities. Teamwork is activated by moving from a "me" mindset to a "we" mindset. Assembling a group of people doesn't mean you have a team. President Woodrow Wilson said, "We should not only use all the brains we have, but all that we can borrow." Teams that work together win together. You need to be in community with those who can band together with you for the cause. The more collaboration that exists, the more creative you will be.

> "Teamwork is only activated by moving from a "me" mindset to a "we" mindset."

DOUBLE DOWN

If you want to see growth, you have to position yourself for it. By preparing yourself and operating in a way which allows for it, growth will happen. Treat what you do as though it is doubled in size; this will force you to think at a higher level and operate in a way that readies you for the increase. What would you need to change if you doubled in size overnight? What systems would need to be more efficient? Who would you need to have in place? Where would you need to put your efforts? If you start to operate in a way that supports this kind of growth, you'll open the door for it to become a reality. Many organizations aren't growing because they aren't set up to handle it. Work in a way which reflects where you want to go, not the way you currently are. Too many times we get so bogged down, maintaining what we have, that we fail to formulate a plan for where we want to go. Begin to operate in a way that stretches you for growth. Double down and function as if you're already there.

REVIEW
5 WAYS TO GET A RAISE
#2 — DO MORE THAN EXPECTED

(2.1) Make It Better
    a) Pursue Excellence
    b) Provide Solutions
    c) Persist Relentlessly

(2.2) Make It Bigger
    a) Push Your Limits
    b) Creatively Collaborate
    c) Double Down

2.3

MAKE IT BRIGHTER

Leaders shine with enthusiasm and cultivate a culture of hope within their organization. One of the greatest military commanders in history, Napoleon Bonaparte, stated, "A leader is a dealer in hope." Unlike the monarchy ruling France during that time, Napoleon understood the importance of winning people over to himself. He knew his soldiers well, calling them by name as he walked through their camps. It is said that Napoleon inspired his soldiers by spending time with them and rewarding their efforts. He believed morale made a significant impact in warfare.

Leaders are hope-dealers. They are continually inspiring people to be, do, and have more. Those who are able to brighten the environment inspire action in others and create more opportunities for themselves.

You may remember the movie Titanic, produced by James Cameron in the late '90s. In the classic scene where the mammoth ship is sinking, a small orchestra is playing music on the deck as the people are clamoring to get into lifeboats. The band continues to play until the very last moments before the ship completely sinks into the Atlantic Ocean. This depiction of the musicians is based on what actually occurred that dreadful night.

The eight-member orchestra was made up of second-class passengers who were contracted out by the British shipping company, White Star Line. They boarded at Southampton, ready to perform their best. Little did they know that this would be their last performance. After the ship hit the iceberg and began to sink, the musicians assembled together to play background music in the lounge to calm the passengers. As the ship sank deeper into the Atlantic, they moved out to the forward half of the boat deck and comforted the masses with beautiful masterpieces as the passengers boarded the lifeboats. All of the musicians went down with the ship, playing until the very end.

In his article, "The Valiant Musicians of the Titanic" Jack Kopstein captured this quote from one of the second class passengers' recounting of the experience, "Many brave things were done that night, but none were more brave than those done by men playing minute after minute as the ship settled quietly lower and lower in the sea. The music they played served alike as their own immortal requiem and their right to be recalled on the scrolls of undying fame." This heroic act of bravery displayed the heart of a true leader. They truly gave their all to create a better environment for the passengers even in the midst of chaos. These men understood the importance of using their ability to make things brighter for those around them.

How can you make things brighter as a leader?

BE PASSIONATE

Ralph Waldo Emerson said, "Enthusiasm is one of the most powerful engines of success. When you do a thing, do it with all your might. Put your whole soul into it. Stamp it with your own personality. Be active, be energetic, be enthusiastic and faithful, and you will accomplish your object. Nothing great was ever achieved without enthusiasm." Passionate people are influencers. They do everything with flair and gusto, not to be noticed but out of genuine love for what they do. If you don't love what you do, you are less likely to achieve success. Passion leads to influence. The more excited you are about your work, the brighter you make the world.

> "The more excited you are about your work, the brighter you make the world."

BE PURPOSEFUL

Leadership is like a connect-the-dots game. In connect-the-dots, you follow a number sequence that turns a seemingly random array of dots into a beautiful design. I was always amazed at how impossible it was to decipher the image before I connected the dots, only to discover the image was there all along, just as intended. In our lives and work, what sometimes appears to be a fragmented mess is actually a beautiful tapestry of opportunity. Great leaders are masters at connecting the dots. They constantly find new ways to bring everyone and everything into harmony. I speak to this in the following excerpt from my book *Leadology*.

If you look closely, you will find that each day will present you with defining moments of opportunity to motivate your team. In the times before modern harbors, a sailor had to wait for the flood tide before they could make it to port with their ship. The Latin phrase "Ob Portu" referred to that moment in time when the tide turned. The captain and crew would wait for that one moment, knowing that if they missed it, they would have to wait for another tide to come in. The English word opportunity derives from this original meaning. Shakespeare used this idea of "Ob Portu" in one of his most famous passages from Julius Caesar:

There is a tide in the affairs of men,
Which, taken at the flood, leads on to fortune;
Omitted, all the voyage of their life
Is bound in shallows and in miseries.
On such a full sea are we now afloat;
And we must take the current when it serves,
Or lose our ventures.

Great leaders are always looking for ways to link daily duties to an overarching vision. They connect every dot to its purpose. They are on the lookout for waves of opportunity to ride.

Are you a connect-the-dots type of leader? Do you look for ways to link common tasks to the overall vision of your organization? The more you can connect the dots for and within your organization, the more you can influence motivation in others to accomplish the vision.

BE POSITIVE

Encouragement is an irresistible form of inspiration. People are influenced to greatness more by those who encourage them than by those who criticize them. The word *encourage* is a compound of the prefix *en*, meaning "to put in or into" and the word *courage*, meaning "confidence and strength." To "encourage" then literally means to put confidence and strength into someone. No one has ever suffered from receiving too much affirmation. When courage resides in someone's heart, they are bolder, stronger, and more effective in all that they do. Their bravery will drive them to overcome any obstacle that may stand in their way. Courage conquers fear and motivates an individual to do things they never thought possible. It pushes them beyond their comfort zones to accomplish great things. Olympic weightlifter, author, and speaker, Jim Stovell said, "You need to be aware of what others are doing, applaud their efforts, acknowledge their successes, and encourage them in their pursuits. When we all help one another, everyone wins."

BE PERSONABLE

Because high achievers are focused on accomplishment, they can easily become hyper-focused on the goal and fail to notice those around them. So busy trying to keep the organization moving forward, they fail to make sure everyone their team is able to keep up with the pace. In the process, they run the risk of losing unity and respect.

> "The more you allow others to shine, the brighter you become."

Don't be like the officer who got so far ahead of the cavalry that he was mistaken for the enemy. It didn't fare well for him, and it won't promise well for you either. Take the time to build strong relationships with those around you, and they will value you more and follow wherever you lead them. Focus on knowing and developing your team. The more you allow others to shine, the brighter you become. Douglas Conant, former President and CEO of Campbell Soup Company, said, "Too many leaders are so caught up in the momentum of work that they lose sight of the opportunity to connect with people. I discovered that the more fully present I was with other people, the more fully present they were with me, and the more productive our relationship became over time."

REVIEW
5 Ways To Get A Raise
#2 — Do More Than Expected

(2.1) Make It Better
    a) Pursue Excellence
    b) Provide Solutions
    c) Persist Relentlessly

(2.2) Make It Bigger
    a) Push Your Limits
    b) Creatively Collaborate
    c) Double Down

(2.3) Make It Brighter
    a) Be Passionate
    b) Be Purposeful
    c) Be Positive
    d) Be Personable

3

WAY #3
EXPLOIT YOUR STRENGTHS

In order to raise your influence, you need to operate from your strengths. Every moment you spend outside of your strength zone is a moment you miss an opportunity to create impact. High capacity achievers do their best to focus on and improve the areas they are great at.

At the 1984 Olympic Games, the Chinese team won the ping-pong gold medal yet again. Curious about their strategy, a reporter asked the team's coach, "Tell me about your team's daily training regimen." He replied, "We practice eight hours a day perfecting our strengths. Here is our philosophy: If you develop your strengths to the maximum, the strength becomes so great it overwhelms the weakness. Our winning player, you see, plays only his forehand. Even though he cannot play backhand–and his competition knows he cannot play backhand–his forehand is so invincible that it cannot be beaten."

Most people think a leader should know everything, is good at everything, and can do everything. This couldn't be further from the truth. In fact, I would argue that it is the complete opposite. A great leader can't possibly know everything, they are only good at a few things, and they certainly don't do all the work by themselves. The longer people buy into this leadership myth, the more detrimental it is. This type of thinking sets one up for a leadership disaster or, at the very least, burnout. To become a valuable player and leader, exploit your greatest strengths. Don't try to be everything, be who you are when you're at your best.

> "To become a valuable player and leader, exploit your greatest strengths."

George Herman Ruth, known as Babe Ruth, played major league baseball from 1914-1935. He started his career as a pitcher for the Red Sox, but later became known as the famous "Bambino Slugger" for the New York Yankees. During the season of 1923, Ruth broke the record for most home-runs. He slammed 60 of them right over the fence. He also broke the record for highest batting average during that same year. What most people do not know is that, during this same season, he also struck out more than any other player in Major League Baseball. And yet, he is not remembered for his strikeouts; he is remembered for being the record-breaking home run hitter. He was so good when he hit the ball that no one focused on his strikeouts.

People will be more impacted by your strengths than your weaknesses. If you want to stand out, find out what you do well and do it as often as you can. When you bring your unique strengths to the table, you'll have a voice in the crowd. Most people are so bogged down doing tasks they're not good at or equipped for that they never get the chance to do what they excel at. According to a recent Gallup report on employee engagement, 50.8% felt as though they were not being utilized to their fullest potential. This is a tragedy. You can't wait for someone to hand you the opportunity to work in your strengths; you have to take the initiative.

Figure out how you can utilize your strengths in every situation. Put your unique touch on what you do. Work on tipping the scale to your strengths, rather than allowing the scale to weigh heavy on your weaknesses.

In 1906, an Italian economist by the name of Vilfredo Pareto discovered a revolutionary pattern. Pareto observed that 20% of the population owned 80% of the land in Italy and that 20% of the pea pods in his garden contained 80% of the peas. This became known as The Law of the Vital Few. We see this law at work in almost every area of life.

- 80 percent of traffic jams occur on 20 percent of the roads.
- 80 percent of classroom participation comes from 20 percent of students.
- 80 percent of the time you wear 20 percent of your clothes.
- 80 percent of the profits come from only 20 percent of the customers.
- 80 percent of problems are generated by 20 percent of the employees.
- 80 percent of sales are generated by 20 percent of the salespeople.
- 80 percent of all decisions can be made on 20 percent of the information.

The same law applies to your strengths. Eighty percent of your impact probably comes from 20% of your effort. It's in that 20% where your strengths lie. So, what if you could flip the scale? What if you could spend 80% of your time working in your strength zone? This would dramatically affect your success. The most successful people spend approximately 80% of their time only doing what only they should be doing.

If you are going to stay in your strength zone, you have to know your strengths, grow your strengths, and show your strengths.

Let's break these down:

EXPLOIT YOUR STRENGTHS

KNOW YOUR STRENGTHS

KNOW YOUR STRENGTHS

"Know Thyself" was written on the forecourt of the Temple of Apollo at Delphi, according to Greek writings. This saying became known all throughout Greek culture as it spread throughout western philosophy. It continues to impact readers and gives us a great starting point for self-awareness today. You have to know yourself in order to grow yourself.

You can only improve that which you are aware of. So, if you are unaware of your strengths, how will you ever be able to improve them? If you haven't identified your target, how can you aim at it? Self-awareness allows you to expedite your influence.

> "Self-awareness allows you to expedite your influence."

Years ago, I dedicated a few months to clearly identifying the strengths I possessed. It was a process of self-discovery as I worked to narrow my focus. I had been increasingly spreading myself thinner and thinner by being involved in too many roles. I finally had to have a meeting with myself to define who I was and where I should be investing my time and effort. Instead of being a jack-of-all-trades-and-master-of-none, I wanted to be a jack-of-few-trades-and-master-of-some. Through self-reflection, I realized there were three areas where I added the most value:

- Communicating
- Coaching
- Creating

I call them my "3C Strength Zone." I realized that these three areas were the places I should be spending at least 80% of my time in and the areas I most needed to grow in. Instead of improving my weaknesses from terrible to average, I decided to improve my strengths from good to great. Instead of winging it in my strength zone, I decided to focus my time and energy there to intentionally develop it. Now, I have a target to aim for each day, and I know where to focus my time and effort. In doing so, I became more valuable to myself and others. When I get out of the 3C Strength Zone, I find myself wasting precious time and diminishing my value and influence. My schedule is now dedicated to spending the majority of my time operating in my strengths.

If I were to ask you, "What are your strengths?" would you have an answer? You should be able to quickly and confidently tell what you do best. If you fumble around or need paragraphs to articulate it, then you don't really know your strengths. If you can't explain what you do best in a few, clear sentences, then you haven't taken the time to know your strengths.

I understand that identifying your strengths can seem difficult to define. When asked what the most difficult thing was, Greek philosopher Thales of Miletus replied, "To know thyself." When asked what was easiest, he replied, "To give advice." It's a lot easier to talk about other people's strengths and weaknesses than to talk about our own. Self-discovery is sometimes a daunting task, but it is necessary for your success. If you don't take the time to know yourself clearly, you won't be able to raise your influential value.

Here are four questions to help you start identifying your strengths.

WHAT ARE YOU PASSIONATE ABOUT?

The areas you are most passionate about usually involve your skills. What do you read about, think about, and ask questions about? These insights will help you know your true passions. Leonardo da Vinci said, "Where the spirit does not work with the hand there is no art." What keeps you up at night because you can't get it off your mind?

WHAT HAVE YOU SUCCEEDED AT IN THE PAST?

You may talk a good game, but what have you successfully accomplished?. What tasks, events, programs, or opportunities have you excelled in? Success in a particular area indicates a level of skill and value. It is hard to excel at things you are bad at. What have you done well, no matter how big or small?

WHAT COMES EASILY TO YOU?

We are naturally intuitive in our area of ability. When you are able to learn a new skill quickly or accomplish specific assignments efficiently, that is usually a good indicator of your strengths. What comes easily to you? What do you accomplish faster than anyone else? What do you inherently understand quicker than others? In what area do you have that "gut feeling" which guides you in your decision making?

WHAT DO YOU MAKE BETTER?

To determine whether or not you are gifted in a particular area, see if you make it bigger or smaller. Highly gifted individuals will take a project and add to it rather than subtract from it. They are more thorough in their efforts and improve the outcome. What things get better once you get a hold of them?

Again, if you want to raise your influence, you have to operate in your strength zone. Discover it, develop it, and discipline yourself to do it.

REVIEW
5 WAYS татоо GET A RAISE
#3 — EXPLOIT YOUR STRENGTHS

(3.1) Know Your Strengths
    a) What Are You Passionate About?
    b) What Have You Succeeded At In The Past?
    c) What Comes Easily To You?
    d) What Do You Make Better?

EXPLOIT YOUR STRENGTHS

GROW YOUR STRENGTHS

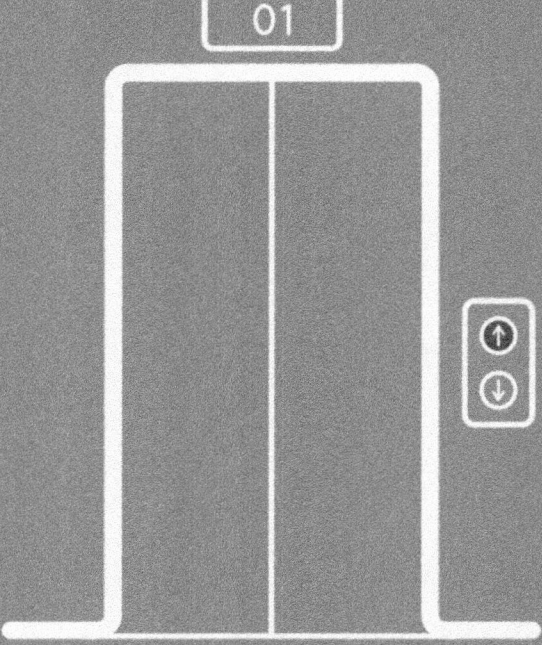

3.2

GROW YOUR STRENGTHS

Growth is not an automatic process. We do not magically get better at the things we do. We only get better when we intentionally grow ourselves. Using your strengths is not the same as growing them. For example, just because you get out of bed in the morning and walk from the bedroom to the bathroom to the kitchen to the dining room doesn't mean you are working out. There is a difference between walking around your house and going on a purposeful, high-intensity walk. Any fitness instructor will tell you that walking during your daily activities is good, but taking time to regularly exercise is infinitely better.

We will only grow to the size that our environment allows. If we place ourselves in environments with only small windows of opportunity and minimal challenges, we will never grow beyond that level. It is when we push ourselves into more challenging situations and environments that our strengths will expand. Just as a fish's growth is restricted by its environment, so too can our environments limit our potential for growth. Who and what you surround yourself with will ultimately determine who you become. If you surround yourself with average people, you will also remain average. If you surround yourself with great leaders, you too will have the potential to become a great leader.

Many people never reach their full potential because they get stuck in an environment lacking in opportunities for growth. When our dreams become bigger than our environment allows, we need to start seeking new terrain. When you plant a tree in a small pot, it will stop growing once it reaches the walls of the pot. The tree is not the problem. It's the environment that is limiting the growth. To grow the tree, you have to put it in an environment that will allow it to develop without borders. Napoleon Hill said, "We begin to see, therefore, the importance of selecting our environment with the greatest of care, because environment is the mental feeding ground out of which the food that goes into our minds is extracted."

If you want to grow your strengths, you have to do more than just use them. You have to decide to strengthen and increase your skills by developing a growth plan. When you raise your abilities, you'll raise your possibilities.

There are three ways you can create a growth environment to develop your strengths and reach your maximum potential.

GET RESOURCES

No one will ever grow to their maximum potential without studying. If you look at the most successful people throughout history, a common trait you will find among them is their insatiable desire for knowledge. It is not surprising to find them studying their craft at the minimum of an hour a day, if not more.

One of the best ways to stimulate the mind is to read. Reading great books, stories, biographies, articles, and blogs pertaining to your strengths is one of the fastest ways to grow on your journey.

Take the wisdom and insights offered by others and apply it to your situation. The mind needs stimulation for transformation. It lets you soar on the wings of other people's great ideas and insights. If you could have spent a month with Steve Jobs for $24.95 would you have? If you could spend a week with Bill Gates for $14.95 would you? If you could spend six months with the top guru in your industry for just $19.95, would you? Well, you can. Grab their books and study their strategies and you'll gain their wisdom.

> "Books are to the mind what nutrition is to the body."

Speaker Earl Nightingale taught that to become an expert in any given field, you must spend one hour a day, every day, for five years studying it. Or, as modern-day author and psychologist Malcolm Gladwell calls it, "The 10,000 Hour Rule." We have to surround ourselves with opportunities for growth. We need to create a growth environment for our strengths to expand.

Books are to the mind what nutrition is to the body. The more you dive into great books, the more growth you'll experience. American philosopher Mortimer Jerome Adler said, "In the case of good books, the point is not how many of them you can get through, but rather how many can get through to you." If you want inspiration, simply read. If you want information, study what you read. If you want transformation, act on what you read. Leaders are readers.

GET MENTORS

You can learn most everything you need in life by being around the right people. Finding mentors who will lift you to a higher level is vital for success. People become like those they surround themselves with. Successful people are drawn to other successful people. They intentionally seek out those who are better and further along than they are themselves. One of the greatest traits of highly successful people is their drive to find and learn from other successful people who are experts in their field. They are excellent networkers who surround themselves with the kind of people they want to become. We cannot reach our potential alone; we need others to both instill and draw out the best in us. Surround yourself with mentors who will add value to your life and encourage you to reach your potential as a leader.

Every great hero had a guide to lead them along the way. Luke had Yoda, Katniss had Haymitch, Frodo had Gandolph, Dorothy had Glenda, Neo had Morpheus, and the list goes on. In the same way, everyone needs a trusted coach to help them unleash the hero they were created to be. In almost every profession, high capacity individuals take advantage of coaching. Movie stars have acting coaches to help them with their roles; singers train their voices with vocal coaches; athletes are guided and instructed by coaches during practices and on game day. Coaches aren't just for beginners. Seasoned professionals make use of coaching for the longevity of their career. The fact is, having a coach helps bring out your very best.

GET EXPERIENCES

All experience is not created equal. Contrary to what you may have heard, experience is not the best teacher; educated experience is. Experience doesn't teach you anything unless you take the time to learn from it. It is not enough to simply go through situations; you have to grow through them. Just because someone goes through a difficult time does not necessarily mean they learned from it. We've all seen people make the same mistakes over and over again. They haven't learned anything from them, and so they continue to make them.

Unless we take the time to reflect upon our experiences, we will be destined to repeat the past, or worse, forget about it. Know that every experience, whether good or bad, has within it a seed of wisdom to impart. Don't waste your experiences. Take the time to evaluate what you have learned from your experiences; it will give you incredible insight for the future. Vernon Howard said, "Always walk through life as if you have something new to learn and you will." It's not what we've experienced that shapes us; it's what we've learned from our experiences that shape us. .

> "It is not enough to simply go through situations; you have to grow through them."

What are you doing to grow your strengths?

REVIEW
5 Ways To Get A Raise
#3 — Exploit Your Strengths

(3.1) Know Your Strengths
      a) What Are You Passionate About?
      b) What Have You Succeeded At In The Past?
      c) What Comes Easily To You?
      d) What Do You Make Better?

(3.2) Grow Your Strengths
      a) Get Resources
      b) Get Mentors
      c) Get Experiences

EXPLOIT YOUR STRENGTHS

SHOW YOUR STRENGTHS

3.3

SHOW YOUR STRENGTHS

In order to gain influence, you have to be willing to show your strengths. Step up and stand out. Be confident in who you are. If you want to be great at what you do, you have to be comfortable with who you are. If you don't value yourself, you will never see value in what you do, and others won't see the value in you.

Showing your strengths requires courage. In fact, the word courage comes from the French word Coeur, meaning "heart." Courage comes from the heart. It takes heart to be a strengths-driven leader. For others to see your creative potential, you have to be courageous enough to put it on display. You will never reach the fullness of your capabilities if you hide your unique abilities. Fear demolishes creative power.

Many people aren't willing to show their unique strengths because of their insecurity. The more insecure a person is, the less courage they have. Their insecurity gives way to fear. Too many people with great ideas and creative talents never share them with the world for fear of what people will think or say. The ability to use your strengths requires you to become vulnerable.

People will always have opinions about your work, but you can't let that keep you from sharing it. What one person considers rubbish may be the gem of inspiration another person needs. Henry

Wadsworth Longfellow said, "Give what you have. To someone, it may be better than you dare to think." Exercise your heart, that courage muscle, and it will continue to get stronger. As you continue to step out and flex your courage, your confidence will grow, and so will your influence.

Here are three tips to help you start releasing your creative potential.

STOP BEING A PERFECTIONIST

Perfectionism whispers in your ear, "You're not ready." When we listen to that lie, our creativity comes to a halt. Break this paralyzing effect by pulling the trigger of courage. Nothing will ever be perfect in this world, so don't wait for it to be. Show your work. Even in its imperfect state, it has something to offer, and in sharing it, you may receive valuable insight into how to make it better. You can't improve a result until you get a result, so just let it go and learn from it. Don't let perfectionism kill your productivity. Perfectionism causes paralysis, which causes procrastination, which causes problems.

Also, if you constantly criticize your work, you will eventually give up in despair. It is okay to think critically about your work; this leads to improvement. However, criticizing your work, much like perfectionism, kills your productivity. Most creative people are not entirely content with what they have produced, but they keep at it, improving their craft along the way. Appreciate your talent, hone it, and grow it. Replace criticism with optimism, and learn to be at peace with your creative efforts.

Embrace Humility

Pride can keep people from showing their work. They become embarrassed by what they've done and allow ego to control them. Humility is a prerequisite to creativity. If you aren't willing to throw yourself out there, you'll never experience the thrill of making a difference. Scientific American held a contest for the best explanation of Einstein's theory of relativity in 3,000 words or less. Einstein said, "I'm the only one in my circle of friends who is not entering. I don't know if I could do it." He truly knew the power of humility. Be humble about your strengths, but be willing to say yes to opportunities that will show them. Author C.S. Lewis said, "Humility is not thinking less of yourself, it's thinking of yourself less."

Don't Be Afraid To Fail

Failure is not always a bad thing; it can actually be the best thing that happens to you. It's all a matter of perspective. You can see failure as a roadblock or a stepping stone…it's your choice. If you see failure as a roadblock, you will avoid it at all costs and eventually come to fear it. However, if you see failure as a stepping stone, you'll feel free to try new things, learning as you stumble and grow. Failure is not fatal; it is simply part of the growth process. The longer you wait to showcase your strengths for fear of failure, the longer it will be until you make a difference in the world.

> "Every failure brings with it the seed of success, but we must extract the lesson in order to grow."

When we stop moving forward for fear of having a bad experience, we miss out on the possibility of having a great experience.

The key to overcoming failure is to keep our eyes forward. Everyone has faced, is facing, or will face failure in their lives. The question is not, "Will I ever fail?" The question is, "How will I respond to failure?" Every failure brings with it the seed of success, but we must extract the lesson in order to grow. Author Tim Fargo said, "Analyze your mistakes. You've already paid the tuition, you might as well get the lesson."

REVIEW
5 WAYS TO GET A RAISE
#3 — EXPLOIT YOUR STRENGTHS

(3.1) Know Your Strengths
    a) What Are You Passionate About?
    b) What Have You Succeeded At In The Past?
    c) What Comes Easily To You?
    d) What Do You Make Better?

(3.2) Grow Your Strengths
    a) Get Resources
    b) Get Mentors
    c) Get Experiences

(3.3) Show Your Strengths
    a) Stop Being A Perfectionist
    b) Embrace Humility
    c) Don't Be Afraid To Fail

(4)

Way #4
Run Up The Score

Growing up in Indiana, it was an unwritten rule that you must love basketball, and I did, especially in elementary school. I'll never forget making the school team the first year I tried out. Fortunately, I was fast and somewhat coordinated, and I seemed to have a natural talent for wielding the leather Spalding ball. My days spent practicing in the driveway at home paid off in the spectator-filled gym.

Not only was I was the top scorer for my team that season, but I also provided the comic relief during games. I was so focused on scoring that every time I made a basket, I would jump up as high as I could and shout, "Yeah!" while throwing my fist in the air with the same intensity that one might throw a punch at their opponent. Every time I sent that ball through the hoop, I looked like I had made the buzzer-beating basket to win the championship game. My enthusiasm never waned, from the first game to the last that entire season. It became my signature move. I was the overly zealous kid who had more enthusiasm for scoring than anyone...probably ever!

All those years playing basketball taught me how important scoring is. I know we've all heard the expression, "It doesn't matter if you win or lose, it's how you play the game." Although there is truth to this perspective, it's only a half-truth. We may give out participation awards in Little League sports, but in life, you have to be in it to win it. Coach Vince Lombardi said, "If it doesn't matter who wins or loses, then why do they keep score?"

As much as character and fortitude matter when you play, in the end it all comes down to the numbers on the scoreboard. A loss is a loss, no matter how you spin it. Economist Milton Friedman once said, "One of the great mistakes is to judge policies and programs by their intentions rather than their results."

> "The more you are able to win, the more opportunities for greatness you'll have."

The scoreboard is the final result...period. Your record of wins and losses determines if you get a shot at the championships. The more you are able to win, the more opportunities for greatness you'll have. Successful people know that all is not lost if you don't win, but you'll have to keep trying until you do.

If you want to increase your influence, you have to put some numbers up on your organization's scoreboard. Note that I didn't say your personal scoreboard. You can do great things, but they have to translate into your organization's success. It's not about you becoming the MVP (most valuable player); it's about helping the organization achieve the MVP (most valuable profit).

Every organization, regardless of industry, seeks a profit. This doesn't always translate into dollars and cents. Profit can look like: changing more lives than it did the year before, delivering better services than it did the year before, or increasing last year's global impact. Whatever the profit goal is, your job is to help your organization accomplish it. Author Mark Sanborn said, "The test of leadership is, is anything or anyone better because of you?" When your contribution assists the overall success of everyone around you, it raises both their value and yours.

If you want to be a starter in the game, you have to be able to run up the score when you're on the court. To help your team win, you need to know the "5 W's" of the scoreboard: Who, What, When, Where, and Why.

RUN UP THE SCORE

WHO

WHO

If you are going to run up points in your organization, you have to know who is in control of the scoreboard. Each one of your clients, colleagues, superiors, board members, owners, etc. has their own personal scoreboard, and if you want to raise your influence, you'll have to know how to win based on their criteria. Great influencers know the art of not only connecting with others but also scoring points with and for them. They are able to both win friends and influence people, as Dale Carnegie taught.

Everyone operates out of their unique personality, which determines what they value. Some are driven by high energy and excitement. Others value calm and consistencies. Then, there are those for whom accuracy and analysis score the most points. You need to know what and who you are working with. Based on their personality, each person will expect different results. For example, Apple founder Steve Jobs was known for his relentless obsession with the look and feel of Apple's products. He wanted everything from product design to packaged delivery to be presented with finesse. He was tenacious about the customer experience starting with opening the box for the very first time to the life-cycle of the product.

You have to know who you are working with in order to accomplish what matters most to them. Study and adapt to the variations of your leaders in order to score greater influence and trust with them. Adjust what you are doing to get the most points possible with those you are dealing with.

Here are some questions to help you identify what people value.

What Makes Them Smile?

It's usually easy to tell when someone is pleased with your work. Some may be more guarded or less responsive, but there's no mistaking when you've scored a point on their scoreboard. You'll see the smile on their face, hear the praise in their voice, or sense a positive shift in their posture towards you. Pay close attention to how they respond to your ideas or projects, and notice the subtle signs they give, clueing you in on what matters most to them. In the same vein, take note as to what doesn't spark their interest. You might work really hard on something that makes no difference at all to them. Don't waste time on things that don't matter or that fail to get points up on the board.

What Do They Repeat?

You know what someone values by how much they talk about it. What do your leaders keep coming back to again and again? Repetition develops reputation. People are known for the things they emphasize. What about you? Are you results driven? Obsessed with golf? Committed to your family? What we consistently do and say reveals who

> "What we consistently do and say reveals who we are and what we value."

we are and what we value. Be cognizant of the words people use, the tone in which they speak, and how often they repeat concepts or values.

What Makes Them Successful?

The more you help others succeed, the more valuable you become to them. What you help others accomplish will also bring you dividends. Zig Ziglar would always say, "You can have everything in life you want, if you will just help other people get what they want." Live with an "others first" mindset, and you'll never lack for opportunity. Educator and presidential advisor Booker T. Washington said, "If you want to lift yourself up, lift up someone else."

REVIEW
5 WAYS TO GET A RAISE
#4 — RUN UP THE SCORE

(4.1) Who
    a) What Makes Them Smile?
    b) What Do They Repeat?
    c) What Makes Them Successful?

RUN UP THE SCORE

WHAT

What

You have to keep your eye on the scoreboard at all times if you want to be successful. Failing to know where you stand can cause you to become either overconfident or undervalued. If you think you are further ahead than you truly are, you might slack off a bit, when you need to be pushing forward. Conversely, if you think you are too far behind to catch up, you may despair, when you should be gaining momentum. Don't make the mistake of turning a blind-eye to the scoreboard at any point in your life.

The scoreboard tells us how we are doing and what we need to be doing. Just as a sports team adjusts their plays according to the score, we too need to adjust our performance based on the score. How can you know what to do if you don't know where you stand?

Beware of organizations that do not have a scoreboard in place to measure their employees' progress. At best, they evaluate their employees at six-month review meetings, only to discover that performance measures should have been put in place months earlier which could have affected certain outcomes. Imagine a team coming into the locker room at half-time and finding out they are 30 points behind. This information would have been beneficial to know during the first half so they could have adjusted their game plan. Great leaders are always pointing to the scoreboard every step of the way.

You may be in an organization that does a great job at keeping the scoreboard at the forefront, but if you aren't, don't get discouraged just yet.

Here's how you can find out what the scoreboard is.

DISCOVER THE SCOREBOARD

If you aren't sure what the scoreboard is, spend some time finding out what matters most to your organization as a whole, by department, and individually. All of these should align with each other, but you may find that your department is shooting on the wrong baskets when you find out what the main focus of the organization is. Don't be afraid to ask questions and seek clarity from those who can give it. You need to be able to determine what a win is so you can know what to shoot for. Author Bill Copeland said, "The trouble with not having a goal is that you can spend your life running up and down the field and never score."

> "You need to be able to determine what a win is so you can know what to shoot for."

DEVELOP YOUR GAME PLAN

Once you know what the scoreboard is, you have to figure out how to get points on it. You need to reverse engineer your goals in order to make sure you know what you're aiming at. For example, if you wanted to lose 20 pounds over the next five months, you'd have to lose four pounds each month, or one pound per week…pretty simple. Based on that plan, you could now begin to measure your progress and see if you are on track. If you don't know what your ultimate weight loss goals are, it's easy to fall into procrastination. You might slack in the middle or forget your weekly goals, and end up having to lose nine pounds in a few weeks because you put your weight loss off. The same is true for any goal you set in life, and especially at work. Make sure you know the game plan before setting up a strategy to win.

Drive Your Performance

Once you know what the scoreboard is and you have a game plan in place with measurable steps, it's time to get on the court and start making some baskets. Every day you should be getting one step closer to winning. Every play should drive you to your target. Every meeting should be purposeful. Every task should align with your organization's values.

When your eyes are fixed on the target, nothing should distract you from it. The word distraction means "to be pulled apart." The word depicts a medieval type of torture method where a person would be pulled apart at the seams of their limbs by being tied to four horses going in opposite directions. This became known as "Death by Dis-traction." We cannot allow ourselves to be distracted from the goals set before us. Everyone faces distractions in life, but the key is to identify them and to move past them. Drive your performance in the straightest line possible to your target by eliminating unnecessary distractions.

REVIEW
5 WAYS TO GET A RAISE
#4 — RUN UP THE SCORE

(4.1) Who
    a) What Makes Them Smile?
    b) What Do They Repeat?
    c) What Makes Them Successful?

(4.2) What
    a) Discover The Scoreboard
    b) Develop Your Game Plan
    c) Drive Your Performance

RUN UP THE SCORE

WHEN

When

Timing is everything when it comes to leveraging your influence.

The proper action done at the improper time causes reluctance.
The improper action done at the proper time causes resistance.
The proper action done at the proper time causes resonance.

When you do something is as important as what you do. There is a rhythm to success. If you want to be successful, then you have to learn how to play in time. Playing too fast or too slow can alter the score dramatically. You have to stay on pace with your team and achieve goals together.

My wife and I went to the beautiful island of Maui on our honeymoon. One of the highlights of our trip was driving "The Road to Hana," which is a famous route that goes around the entire island. It took us about three hours to complete the route in our rented Ford Escort. About halfway through the journey, we pulled over at the top of a cliff to watch the windsurfers out on the ocean. It was incredible to see these people doing all kinds of tricks and moves on the waves. Periodically, there would be moments of calm on the water when the waves died down. The surfers would then wait for the next big wave as they floated in the water. As I watched, I observed how much surfing is based on momentum. Even the best surfers in the world are limited by seas which become as smooth as glass. These surfers certainly had the skills and potential to perform incredible tricks, but they were restricted by the lack of wind and waves. They didn't get discouraged and give up when the waves died down; they were patient, knowing that more were on the way. And, as soon as the waves started to come in again, they were up and surfing.

Influencers are like surfers: they are momentum seekers. They look for ways to catch opportunities which will create momentum and put points on the scoreboard. A professional surfer will calmly wait for the perfect wave to come along. They know how to read the waves and determine which will offer the best opportunity. Many times, a surfer will pass on a perfectly good wave in order to catch a great wave, and when they see it, they quickly paddle out and seize the moment. Therein lays momentum. It is in that pivotal moment that they find the momentum which will carry them to new, daring heights.

Momentum is your ally. When you have momentum on your side, everything you do seems to work. Momentum makes you look better than they are. Momentum puts wind in your sails. It enables you to go further and faster. It takes your team and your organization to greater places. When you have momentum on your side, it feels like nothing can stop you. You dream bigger and are willing to risk more.

However, where there is a lack of momentum, even the best ideas have difficulty gaining traction. Lack of momentum is a person's worst enemy. It makes someone look worse than they really are. It is very difficult to move forward without momentum.

So how can you spot and catch these waves of momentum?

BE A PROFESSIONAL OBSERVER

Study how people think and operate. The better you understand people, the easier it will be to connect with them. People are like chess pieces, not checkers. In checkers, you treat every piece the same. But in chess, you have to be aware of how each piece uniquely functions in order to win. Failing to understand how people operate can be the difference between winning and losing.

> "Failing to understand how people operate can be the difference between winning and losing."

BE A PROFESSIONAL TESTER

Most people assume there is a predetermined formula for success, but it is really the result of trial and error that leads to eventual success. Just look at Thomas Edison. Still, we imagine that success is some elusive objective reserved for the elite few. Reject this myth, and start thinking outside the box. Dare to try something new. If at first, you don't succeed, try, try again. Remember, you first have to get a result in order to improve the result. Tinker with new ideas, new systems, and new opportunities. Test the best ways to put points on the board.

BE A PROFESSIONAL OPTIMIST

FOMO (Fear Of Missing Out) is a cultural buzzword of the day. People are plagued with the feeling they are on the outside looking in. FOMO is an anxiety-inducing stressor which leads to poor decision making. It causes a play now, pay later cycle of life. Don't fall prey to its deceitful charms. Instead, be led by

FIFO: Faith In Future Opportunities. FIFO encourages you to activate self-discipline by believing that there is something better in store for the future than what you see before you right now. People with a strong sense of FIFO will pay now in order to play later. In doing so, they have a much greater level of influence than those who suffer from FOMO. They look to the future with optimism and hope, which helps them to deny their desire for instant gratification in favor of future greatness.

REVIEW

5 WAYS TO GET A RAISE
#4 — RUN UP THE SCORE

(4.1) Who
    a) What Makes Them Smile?
    b) What Do They Repeat?
    c) What Makes Them Successful?

(4.2) What
    a) Discover The Scoreboard
    b) Develop Your Game Plan
    c) Drive Your Performance

(4.3) When
    a) Be A Professional Observer
    b) Be A Professional Tester
    c) Be A Professional Optimist

RUN UP THE SCORE

WHERE

WHERE

In order to score big, you have to know where the basket is. You can't do an alley-oop or make a slam dunk if you can't find the hoop. On the court, the baskets stay put, but in life, they are constantly shifting and changing. Just take a look at these computer terms which once had common, everyday meanings.

- Window: something you opened to let fresh air in
- Ram: cousin of a goat
- Meg: name of someone's girlfriend
- Gig: a nightclub job
- App(lication): the form you filled out for employment
- Program: a TV show
- Cursor: someone who used profanity
- Keyboard: part of a piano
- Memory: a function of the brain
- CD: a type of bank account
- Compress: something you did to the garbage
- Unzip: something you did to your jacket or pants.
- Log on: as in "put another log on the fire"
- Hard drive: a long, difficult road trip.
- Mousepad: where a mouse lived
- Backup: something that happened to your commode or during rush hour

- Cut: something you did with scissors or a pocket knife
- Paste: something you did with glue
- Web: a spider's home.
- Virus: something that plagued the body, like the flu.

Everything changes over time. Just look at how different things are from when you were young. In the same way, your organization will also change. What works now will need updating or alteration in the future. Culture changes. Market conditions change. People change. Wants and needs change. Leadership expert and author John P. Kotter said, "The rate of change is not going to slow down anytime soon. If anything, competition in most industries will probably speed up even more in the next few decades."

Sometimes trying to score points is like aiming at a moving target. How you respond to the ever-changing environment will determine your level of success. You can either be angry about the change, or you can adapt to it—the choice is yours. Those who can successfully navigate change with a positive perspective are those who will become invaluable in the long run. Your speed of adapting to change will determine your rate of success.

In 1906, American football changed forever. The forward pass was legalized, but no one adopted this new strategy. They clung to their traditional methods of running and kicking the ball. However, St. Louis University practiced the new play and implemented it that season. They outscored their opponents 402 to 11 that year and changed the game forever. Instead of resisting the new rule, they adapted their gameplay, and it resulted in big wins for them.

If you are going to navigate change and keep scoring points even with a moving target, you need to do these three things:

STAY CURRENT

My good friend Chris Page once said, "If you don't update you'll outdate." I couldn't agree more. If you don't stay in the stream of progress, you'll dissipate in a puddle of decay. You have to stay focused on the future to keep pace in the present. In the early 2000's, Blockbuster Video had the opportunity to buy out Netflix for just $50 million. This was small change for the 5.9 billion dollar empire, but they rejected the opportunity because they didn't believe there was a market for Internet-based video. Not long after, Blockbuster declared bankruptcy as Netflix experienced meteoric success leading to its present-day $32.9 billion value. French poet Victor Hugo said, "The future has several names. For the weak, it is impossible. For the fainthearted, it is unknown, but for the valiant, it is ideal."

> "If you don't stay in the stream of progress, you'll dissipate in a puddle of decay."

STAY CULTIVATED

American futurist and writer Alvin Toffler said, "The illiterate of the 21st century will not be those who cannot read and write, but those who cannot learn, unlearn, and relearn." We must commit ourselves to stay on top of our game. Just as an athlete must train in the off-season to stay agile, we too must remain committed to excellence in season and out. Cultivate an endurance-mindset which helps you stay patient through the challenges of change and determined to rise with the tide. Remember the old statement: "Trouble is inevitable, but misery is optional." Gymnast

Dan Millman said, "The secret of change is to focus all your energy not on fighting the old, but on building the new."

STAY CURIOUS

The famous artist Picasso said, "Every child is an artist. The problem is how to remain an artist once we grow up." He reinforced this truth when he remarked, "It took me four years to paint like Raphael, but a lifetime to paint like a child." What Picasso knew and almost all highly successful people know is that you must never lose your child-like curiosity. The moment you stop growing is the moment you start dying. When we are young, our minds are like sponges, always eager to learn something new. As we grow older, though, we turn into critics and become cynical about new ideas and cultural changes. Don't let your inner critic override your sense of childlike wonder. Keep asking questions and look with hope to the future. Walt Disney said, "We keep moving forward, opening new doors, and doing new things, because we're curious and curiosity keeps leading us down new paths."

REVIEW
5 WAYS TO GET A RAISE
#4 — RUN UP THE SCORE

(4.1) Who
    a) What Makes Them Smile?
    b) What Do They Repeat?
    c) What Makes Them Successful?

(4.2) What
    a) Discover The Scoreboard
    b) Develop Your Game Plan
    c) Drive Your Performance

(4.3) When
    a) Be A Professional Observer
    b) Be A Professional Tester
    c) Be A Professional Optimist

(4.4) Where
    a) Stay Current
    b) Stay Cultivated
    c) Stay Curious

[RUN UP THE SCORE]

WHY

WHY

We've explored the importance of the scoreboard in terms of who, what, when, and where, but without a why, all else is futile. Here are three reasons why the scoreboard is essential to success.

WHERE YOU'VE BEEN

If you don't know the score, how do you know whether you are making a positive or negative impact on the court? Scoreboards help you measure your progress from past to present. Sports teams always start at zero and build from that common starting point. If you don't know what your starting point is, how can you determine your progress?

The scoreboard is vital to measuring success. Organizations that don't have a scoreboard can only guess at how they and their employees are actually doing. The problem with guessing is that it is subjective to emotions, opinions, challenges, and changes, all of which can change from day to day. The scoreboard is an impartial marker of progress. You may be running up and down the court, feeling like you've expended every last ounce of energy, but if you haven't made a basket, you aren't making a positive impact on the game. Whatever the scoreboard shows, it is vital to know where you stand, both individually and as a team. Coach Lou Holtz said, "We aren't where we want to be; we aren't where we ought to be; but thank goodness we aren't where we used to be."

Author Max De Pree said, "The first responsibility of a leader is to define reality." You can't manage what you don't measure. There is no unity until there is a standard. Too many people and organizations operate from unclear expectations. How can you hold people accountable to a conceptual abstraction? You can't. Unclear expectations produce unmet results. You can only ensure accountability with concrete metrics. Scoreboards give a clear picture of what the real score is, not someone's arbitrary idea of it.

> "Unclear expectations produce unmet results."

WHERE YOU'RE AT

Knowing where you are in relation to the scoreboard allows you to make the necessary adjustments for greater impact. Every decision should be made in consultation with the scoreboard. As you move forward, keep your eye on the scoreboard to measure your progress and change your course as needed. Avoiding the scoreboard for fear of failure will not lead to success. Use the scoreboard as a motivator either to praise forward progress or to suggest changes leading to advancement. Either way, knowing where you're at on the scoreboard gives you an opportunity to influence the outcome rather than just hoping it turns out right in the end. Soccer player Alex Morgan said, "Always work hard, never give up, and fight until the end because it's never really over until the whistle blows."

WHERE YOU'RE GOING

When you look at the scoreboard, you gain valuable insight into how to plan for the future. All of your goals should be derived from the analysis of the scoreboard. Use them to project out and identify trends resulting from your efforts. Present patterns determine future outcomes. When you hit record highs, don't become complacent; keep pushing for further success.

On May 6th, 1954 Roger Bannister ran the first under-4-minute mile. Previous to this accomplishment, doctors said it could not be done. They believed the human heart would explode from such extreme activity. Amazingly six weeks after Bannister accomplished that feat, an Australian runner duplicated it. The following year, eight college runners, all at the same track meet, broke the four-minute mile. Be a record breaker, and set the mark for future success. When you have a target to shoot for, you increase your chances for victory. Hockey player Wayne Gretzky said, "A good hockey player plays where the puck is. A great hockey player plays where the puck is going to be." Keep your eyes forward and stretch yourself to better results.

REVIEW
5 WAYS TO GET A RAISE
#4 — RUN UP THE SCORE

(4.1) Who
    a) What Makes Them Smile?
    b) What Do They Repeat?
    c) What Makes Them Successful?

(4.2) What
    a) Discover The Scoreboard
    b) Develop Your Game Plan
    c) Drive Your Performance

(4.3) When
    a) Be A Professional Observer
    b) Be A Professional Tester
    c) Be A Professional Optimist

(4.4) Where
    a) Stay Current
    b) Stay Cultivated
    c) Stay Curious

(4.5) Why
    a) Where You've Been
    b) Where You're At
    c) Where You're Going

Way #5
Lead Yourself

The hardest person you will ever lead is…yourself.

President Theodore Roosevelt once stated, "If you could kick the person in the pants responsible for most of your trouble, you wouldn't sit for a month." You are either your best friend or your worst enemy. You will never get the most out of your life if you don't learn to lead yourself. Let's break down the word leadership: lead-er-ship…lead-ur-ship…lead-yur-ship…lead-your-ship. You have to lead your ship if you want to sail to great destinations.

When we come to accept responsibility for the leadership of our lives, we will begin to take the first steps toward greatness. Remember, leadership is more about who you are than what you do. It is an inward decision that results in outward expression. Forget about leading the masses if you can't lead yourself. Forget about inspiring others if you can't inspire yourself. Forget about getting a raise if you can't raise your abilities. Thomas J. Watson, the former chairman and CEO of IBM said, "Nothing so conclusively proves a man's ability to lead others as what he does from day to day to lead himself."

Every day, you bring a version of yourself to work. It's your choice who that person will be. Will it be the best version of yourself, the worst version of yourself, or the caught-in-the-middle version of yourself? Situations may dictate which version you bring on any given day, but to achieve success, we must strive to bring the boldest, most focused, and highly energized version of ourselves to all that we do. When we are truly present, we have the potential to become great influencers. When we are focused on the end goal, we become unstoppable on the path to success. Not only will we inspire ourselves to action each day, but we will also inspire others to action. When you inspire others, you raise your level of influence and increase your impact on the overall organization, which will also raise your income.

There are three things we need to do to lead ourselves effectively: remember, resolve, and retreat. Let's break these down.

[LEAD YOURSELF]

REMEMBER

5.1

REMEMBER

Government official Paul Nitze said, "One of the most dangerous forms of human error is forgetting what one is trying to achieve." It's not what we don't know that holds us back; it's what we know but don't do. I have coached many people over the years, and the one common trait that successful clients share is their need to be reminded of what they already know to do. It's not a matter of ignorance; it's simply a matter of forgetting.

You see, most of us already have a sense of what it would take for our lives, businesses, relationships, or projects to go to the next level. We're not completely at a loss; we're just overwhelmed by the vortex of busyness which makes us forget what we need to be doing. The rat race of life gets the best of us, and our vision becomes blurry. Our enthusiasm wanes as we strive to achieve but lose sight of the goal.

It is essential that you remain intentional about who you are and where you are going. Knowing why you are doing what you're doing is vital to success. When you lose your why, you'll begin to lose your way.

Like a heat-seeking missile that is continuously course-correcting in order to lock on its target, we also need to keep ourselves on track. Jonas Salk, the man who developed the polio vaccine, said, "Life is an error-making and error-correcting process." I wholeheartedly agree with that statement and would add that leadership operates by the same principle. The goal is to keep ourselves pointed to true north as we navigate through all the challenges of life. Yes, you will get off course at times...that is inevitable. But, if you build guardrails along the path of your life, they will keep you from driving off a cliff and redirect you back on course to attaining your goals. (On a side note, if you don't have clarity on the big picture for your life, you need to get one. Check out the book *Living Forward* by Michael Hyatt, or author Simon Sinek's book *Find Your Why* to work through a life plan.)

When you identify your purpose, you will achieve PHD for your future, which stands for: Perspective...Hope...Direction

Perspective

Perspective allows us to see things that we otherwise wouldn't be able to see. If you were to look ahead from where you stand now, your view would be blocked by various obstacles in front of you (i.e. trees, buildings, etc.). However, if you were to climb up a tree, you would have a view above those obstacles. You would have a clearer perspective of the path ahead.

We gain perspective by seeing things through the eyes of purpose. It gives us a bird's eye view of why we are doing what we are doing. It's much easier to endure difficulties when we know there is a light at the end of tunnel...and, no, it's not a train heading our way for a collision.

Hold the image of the things you desire to accomplish before you, and before you know it, they will become a reality. I held the image of impacting people's lives and inspiring them by speaking to large crowds long before I ever had the opportunity to do so. I held the image of starting a business long before I had the means to. I held the image of being married to a beautiful woman, inside and out, long before I married my wife. I held the image of writing books long before I ever put a word down on paper. George Lucas said, "Dreams are extremely important. You can't do it unless you can imagine it." The moment you lose sight of your dreams is the moment you'll stop pursuing them.

> "The moment you lose sight of your dreams is the moment you'll stop pursuing them."

Perspective changes everything. Have you ever seen a holographic picture? When you stand just in the right place, an abstract picture would change into a beautiful scene before your very eyes. But, you had to get the exact perspective in order for the image to become clearly visible. Life works in much the same way. Many times we see situations out of focus; they become blurred by our emotional responses or poor judgment. We have lost our sense of perspective. Sometimes, all it takes is taking a step back to see the whole picture to regain a proper perspective.

HOPE

When asked about his country's greatest weapon against the Nazi regime, Winston Churchill didn't hesitate to respond, "It was what England's greatest weapon had always been… hope."

What Churchill knew, and what all great leaders know, is that the most empowering gift a person can receive is hope. It is unquestionably the strongest motivational force in all the earth. When hope fills our heart, we are able to dream of a better future. We begin to see possibilities that we couldn't see before. The impossible becomes possible.

The courageous exploits of every explorer were based on the hopeful belief that something better existed in the great beyond. Without it, no one would have ventured into uncharted territory.

Hope motivates the unlikeliest people to do the most unlikely things in the most unlikely ways. Hope-giving leaders are forward-focused, and they instill that positive energy into their organization's culture. Instead of dwelling on yesterday's mistakes, have hope for tomorrow and prepare for future possibilities.

Our country was founded on the premise of an unwavering hope for a new life and a greater future. In the journal of Christopher Columbus during his first voyage to America, there was an entry that read, "The sea will grant each man new hope, the sleep brings dreams of home." When Christopher Columbus set sail in 1492, his flagship, the Santa Maria, carried the flag of Queen Isabella. That flag had the image of a castle on it, along with the inscription "Ne Plus Ultra," meaning "nothing further." At the time, Spain was considered the most western part of the world. When Columbus returned to Spain and reported his findings to the queen, she ordered a painter to change the flag to read "Plus Ultra," which means "more beyond" or "more out there." Hope believes there is more to come. It is when we lose sight of the possibilities that we begin to wither away inside. Show me a person with no hope, and I will show you someone who will eventually give up on their pursuits.

DIRECTION

Having a clear sense of direction is a great filter to determine whether or not you are spending your time and energy in the right way. A million voices call us to go this way or that way. If we're not careful, we can get caught up in the whirlwind of chaos or get lost in the wilderness of busyness. We are prone to what I call situation disorientation. This happens when we forget where we are headed and fall victim to irrelevant distractions. Holocaust survivor Viktor Frankl said, "Without a clear purpose any obstacle will send a person in a new direction." Your purpose determines your direction.

Direction is essential to achieving our goals. The clock doesn't determine your productivity; your internal compass does. If what you are doing with your time doesn't align with your purpose, you will be headed in the wrong direction. You can be busy doing all the wrong things, or worse, you can be productive in all the wrong areas. Your internal compass guides your schedule and keeps you in line with your purpose.

There are three ways people navigate their time. They are either victims of their time, managers of their time, or leaders of their time.

VICTIMS OF TIME

These people are beat down and knocked out by their schedules. They cannot say no to anything or anyone, and their lives are cluttered with the "stuff" of consumption. With no boundaries or defenses against the time stealers robbing them of their productivity, they over-schedule themselves with more than they can handle. Victims need to learn how to stand up and defend their time, or excessive commitments will destroy them.

MANAGERS OF TIME

These people are barely keeping their heads above water as they tread back and forth. They are not getting ahead in life; they are simply maintaining what they have. Managers live on the brink of chaos. They focus on keeping the ship afloat and spend most their time dumping out the excess water that keeps splashing onboard. These people deceive themselves by thinking that if they are managing their time they are being productive when the truth is they are not producing anything. They never have time to pursue their purpose because they are always dealing with the urgent demands of life, which suck up all their time and energy.

LEADERS OF TIME

These people know how to make time work for them. They control their time; their time doesn't control them. They are focused on what really matters and yield a fruitful harvest from their labor. They do not waste their time on urgent, or even good, things. Instead, they commit their time to those things that line up directly with their purpose. The rest they delegate to others, or they surrender them altogether. Leaders live with focus and purpose, doing what they are "called" to do.

Every day counts, so make the most of it and aspire to be a leader of your time.

REVIEW
5 WAYS TO GET A RAISE
#5 — LEAD YOURSELF

(5.1) Remember
    a) Perspective
    b) Hope
    c) Direction
          - Victims of Time
          - Managers of Time
          - Leaders of Time

LEAD YOURSELF

RESOLVE

5.2

RESOLVE

In order to lead yourself, you need to live with resolve. Be the kind of person who gets stuff done. Anyone can start something, but it's those who can finish a task that become successful. The first mile of a marathon is crowded, but those who make it to the last mile have a wide open path to the finish line. Seeing things through to completion is a sign of strong leadership. Author Jeff Goins said, "Don't waste your time with writing resolutions this New Year. Instead, focus on something else: resolve. While the words are similar, the difference in meaning is significant. A resolution is something you make. Resolve is something you have. In other words, commit. Choose into a process, not a set of audacious goals you'll never meet."

When I taught my youngest daughter how to ride I bike, I saw the difference between retreat and resolve. Every time she began to feel the slightest tilt of imbalance, my daughter would immediately jump off her bike in mid-flight. This became a habit she developed through repetition. The moment fear crept in, she would yell, "I'm bailing!" I kept encouraging her not to bail, but she kept giving into her insecurity. Over time, we eventually overcame that hurdle, as she learned how to manage her balance. Her resolve grew until she finally harnessed the power of staying on the bike, even when she felt unsteady.

My daughter isn't the only one who is tempted to bail at the first sign of danger or uncertainty. This is a common, human response. Fear conditions us to jump ship at the first sign of discomfort. In fact, the word *fear* comes from the Old English word *faer*, meaning "sudden ambush or attack." That is exactly what fear does: it attacks our courage and causes us to shrink back from following through.

You will never rise up to your potential unless you resolve to push through your fears. The moment we give in to our fears is the moment we cease growing. All true progress takes place just beyond the borders of fear. Successful people don't run from fear; they run through it. They gain courage by facing their fears head-on.

The path of potential runs straight through the heart of fear. You can't achieve your purpose without breaking through the fear barrier. Sadly, most people never meet their potential because they turn back or take a detour away from fear. They never experience the satisfaction of facing their fears and achieving their goals, which leads to lives of complacency, or worse, regret. You have to get comfortable with feeling uncomfortable in order to live a life of significance.

In my early 20's, I worked a side-job at a shipping center. One of my co-workers was an amateur boxer. Each day that I came to work, he would share boxing tips he was learning with me. Looking back, I realized that some of the principles he taught me apply to our life journey, as well. There are three great parallels I found between the resolve a boxer must have and the resolve we all need to have: prepare yourself, position yourself, and pace yourself.

PREPARE YOURSELF

The fight begins way before the fight begins. If we are going to win in life, we must understand that the majority of the battle is won outside of the ring. Heavyweight champion Joe Frazier said, "You can map out a fight plan or a life plan, but when the action starts, it may not go the way you planned, and you're down to your reflexes—that means your preparation. That's where your road-work shows. If you cheated on that in the dark of the morning, well, you're going to get found out now, under the bright lights."

Our time in the ring exposes how well we have trained. If we take shortcuts and slack off, we will not be able to contend with our opponent (i.e. life's challenges). You may have heard the saying, "When preparation meets opportunity, there is success," but the opposite, "When procrastination meets opportunity, there is distress," is also true. Preparing on the front end helps us be victorious on the back end.

> "Preparing on the front end helps us be victorious on the back end."

It's hard to be resolute when you aren't prepared for what's ahead of you. Preparation creates confidence. Procrastination breeds chaos. Unplanned time leads to an unproductive life. The truth still remains...if you fail to plan, you plan to fail. I coach many people who have lost their edge because they are coasting rather than creating. They are victims of procrastination; therefore they experience disorientation when it comes to their agenda. They have so much to do, and no sense of direction, that they become overwhelmed and get nothing done.

Keep in mind that the more you have to do, the more you must plan how you are going to do it. Benjamin Franklin said, "For every minute spent organizing, an hour is earned." The greatest enemy of success is wasted time. Don't waste precious time on non-precious things. Some common time wasters are: watching too much T.V., sleeping in, daydreaming, lounging, and surfing social media. These activities kill your productivity. Get busy preparing yourself for a better tomorrow.

- If you exercise today you will be healthier tomorrow.
- If you make money today you will have something tomorrow.
- If you work on a project today you will be one step closer to finishing it tomorrow.
- If you read today you will be closer to finishing the book tomorrow.
- If you practice your skill today you will be closer to mastering that skill tomorrow.
- If you put gas in the tank today you don't have to fill it tomorrow.
- If you have the "meeting" today you can move on tomorrow.
- If you forgive yourself and others today you can walk in freedom tomorrow.
- If you think today then you will have a plan for tomorrow.
- If you love others today you will have relationships with you tomorrow.
- If you spend time with your kids today you will have respect from them tomorrow.

Position Yourself

Keep moving forward. Don't stop. You will never see a professional boxer standing still in the ring. They keep moving to keep their blood flowing, position themselves better, and stay light on their feet. The worst thing you can do during a challenging time is to get stuck in it. When we stop moving is when we become the most vulnerable. Winston Churchill said, "If you're going through hell, keep going." The Prime Minister knew that whenever you stop moving, especially in a fight, you are more likely to get knocked out. Instead of retreating into your own fears and hurt, convincing yourself that you can't go on, continue to advance. It is only as you propel yourself forward that you push through the pain and win the fight. You cannot fight complacency by being complacent, and you do not fight fatigue by remaining fatigued. To win in life, you have to discipline yourself to keep repositioning by staying in motion.

Remember Newton's law of motion: An object at rest stays at rest, and an object in motion stays in motion with the same speed and in the same direction unless acted upon by an unbalanced force. When you keep moving forward, you'll always be advancing towards success. But the moment you let an outside force waylay your momentum, you become more susceptible to defeat. Just like a boxer has to protect himself from his opponent's punches, so you must protect yourself from all the forces that will try to impede your progress. The path to success is not a short open sprint; it's a marathon filled with hurdles. Keep a steady pace to make it to the end. Through various trials: resistance, complacency, and distractions keep moving forward. The only way you will make it to the end is by taking it one day at a time. I came across this picture that captures exactly how we want the journey to look like versus how it actually is:

> "The path to success is not a short open sprint; it's a marathon filled with hurdles."

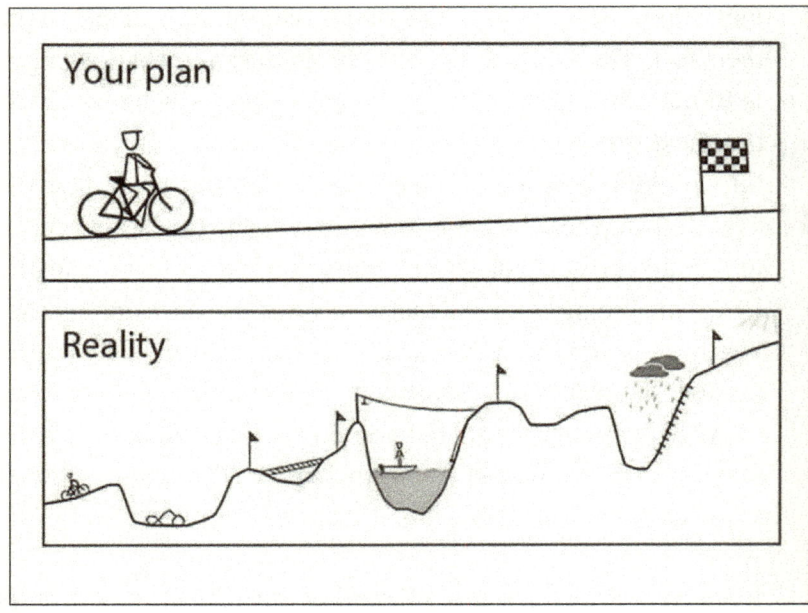

You must break through the obstacles that stand in your way if you want to reach the pinnacle of your dreams. Never allow your fear to halt your progress. Instead, always position yourself for forward movement.

PACE YOURSELF

Don't go for the knockout right away. Boxers who go in for the knockout as soon as the bell rings usually end up knocking themselves out later in the fight. Why? Because they did not pace themselves correctly and consequently ran out of energy. Boxing is all about controlling your rhythm. And rhythm is all about timing.

Impatience causes us to miss out on our best efforts. We win the fight by building up our endurance for the journey. Endurance plus courage keeps us in the fight to the final bell. Johnny Nguyen, the founder of Expert Boxing, said, "Being able to relax in stressful environments allows you to make smart decisions and benefit more out of the situation. Slow down and look around so you can absorb everything. If you're always pushing yourself over the limit, you'll end up making yourself quit, and this attitude will show in everything that you do. You are your own worst enemy." Johnny's advice stands true for our everyday lives, as well. It is like the old saying goes, "You get a chicken by hatching the egg, not by smashing it."

If you want to have a sustainable level of success, you have to be patient. Things always take longer than you thought and are harder than you anticipated. Without the discipline of patience, you will give up and bail on your pursuit of success. Thinking you will be an overnight success is not reality. I once heard it said that anyone can become an overnight success after 20 years of hard work.

Success is a daily process of pressing on even when it gets tough. Patience and endurance work together in this regard. Endurance is the ability to have patience, and patience is the ability to endure. Philosopher Thomas Carlyle said, "Endurance is patience concentrated." Remember The Tortoise and the Hare: "Slow and steady wins the race."

William Arthur Ward wrote these great words of advice:

>Believe while others are doubting
>Plan while others are playing
>Study while others are sleeping.
>Decide while others are delaying

Prepare while others are daydreaming
Begin while others are procrastination
Work while others are wishing
Save while others are wasting
Listen while others are talking
Smile while others are frowning
Commend while others are criticizing
Persist while others are quitting

Hang in there and never give up. Keep moving and throwing punch after punch.

REVIEW
5 WAYS TO GET A RAISE
#5 — LEAD YOURSELF

(5.1) Remember
      a) Perspective
      b) Hope
      c) Direction
            - Victims of Time
            - Managers of Time
            - Leaders of Time

(5.2) Resolve
      a) Prepare Yourself
      b) Position Yourself
      c) Pace Yourself

LEAD YOURSELF

RETREAT

5.3

RETREAT

In the book The Making of a Corporate Athlete, Jim Loehr and Tony Schwartz explained how they spent years training and developing Olympic athletes in performance management. This led them to the corporate world where they trained world-class leaders in productivity with the same principles they taught athletes. They made a significant impact on the efficiency of many organizations by enhancing employee performance. They wrote this about the importance of balance:

"In a corporate environment that is changing at warp speed, performing consistently at high levels is more difficult and more necessary than ever. Narrow interventions simply aren't sufficient anymore. Companies can't afford to address their employees' cognitive capacities while ignoring their physical, emotional, and spiritual well-being. On the playing field or in the boardroom, high performance depends as much on how people renew and recover energy as on how they expend it, on how they manage their lives as much as on how they manage their work. When people feel strong and resilient—physically, mentally, emotionally, and spiritually—they perform better and longer, with more passion. They win, their families win, and the corporations that employ them win."

According to their research and real-life applications, the whole key to performance rests on the ability to renew and recover from stress. The rhythm of productivity hinges not just on what you do, but also on what you don't do. Taking time to refresh enhances your productivity for when you are working.

This is seen in every aspect of life. For example, there is a very effective form of physical exercise called high-intensity interval training. This training is based on the science that our bodies are designed to function optimally when they are subject to short bursts of energy followed by moments of recovery. This approach can be applied to our emotional and mental health, too.

GET SELFISH

Taking time for yourself is essential if you want to be successful. Sometimes, you have to get selfish if you are going to achieve a healthy balance of work and recovery. Always giving without receiving eventually leads to burnout. Most people's life ratios today look like 9:1 output, leaving a 1:9 input.

You can only output what you have inputted. You cannot give what you do not have. Blocks happen when you have not inputted enough for it to overflow out of you. It is not that you are uninspired, lazy, indecisive, or even stuck; you simply have not filled your energy tank with enough juice. When you are inputting time for rest and rejuvenation, you will output greater stamina. Productivity is an overflow of what we have put inside us.

Always outputting and never inputting will be your ultimate downfall. Relationships will suffer, productivity will suffer, health will suffer, and you will suffer from not having a well-balanced life. We need to shoot more for a 1:1 ratio of output and input, meaning, that for every time you extract a large amount of energy, you need to refuel your tank. If you study some of the most successful people, you will find they have created vast amounts of margin in their schedule to recover and replenish their energy. Still, for some reason, we believe the lie that, in order to be productive and successful, you must work 65+ hours a week. Reject that myth and make sure you are scheduling in margin along with all of your other responsibilities.

You must be mentally and physically prepared for the opportunities that come your way, and margin is the way to allow for this. Margin is the white space in our lives and on our calendars: the time we set aside for rest, creativity, quiet. Living with no margin leads to burnout. Is your schedule over-filled? It's time to take something(s) off your plate. It's impossible to manage a life without margin; you have to figure out what to release to make room for white space, which is as essential as any other scheduled item in your life. Remember, for every one thing you add to your schedule, you need to subtract another thing. For every yes, there is also be a no. Identifying what is truly important in life is the key to deciding what remains and what goes.

Are you going to bed too late, waking up too early, racing out the door, always running behind schedule? You can't stay on top of things when you are always playing catch up. Be intentional about scheduling breaks between meetings and downtime throughout your week. Make space for your imagination to expand, through creative endeavors.

GET HOBBIES

Follow the example of successful people throughout history: get a hobby. Here are some of their hobbies:

- Former President George W. Bush is an avid painter
- Actress Susan Sarandon calls herself a ping-pong propagandist
- Billionaire Richard Branson's favorite sport is kiteboarding
- Investor Warren Buffet plays a lot of online bridge
- Inventor Albert Einstein loved to sail
- Apple founder Steve Jobs played guitar
- Actress Angelina Jolie collects daggers
- Google co-founder Sergey Brin does trapeze

Hobbies allow us to escape from work and replenish our quality of life. All work plus no play equals psychological disarray. When we engage in an enjoyable hobby, we are investing in our well-being. Having healthy creative outlets allows us to decompress from stress. Everyone should have a hobby that they can get lost in at times. The oscillation from work to play generates more creative energy. Remember playing cars as a kid with Hot Wheels, micro-machines, or whatever type of toy you had? You could set up tracks with three-hundred-sixty-degree loops right in the middle.

> "All work plus no play equals psychological disarray."

These loops would create momentum for the car to keep going until it reached the finish line. As soon as the car made its way down the loop, it would pick up an extreme amount of force to keep moving. In the same way, hobbies create a propelling loop that gives us the mental and physical strength to keep persevering. They reward us with improved creativity, emotional restoration, self-confidence, stress relief, social connection, idea generating, leadership lessons, and broader awareness. Simply put, hobbies are extremely good for the soul and the mind.

So many world-changing ideas and solutions have been conceived during recreation. For instance, 3M inventor Art Fry had his breakthrough moment while on the companies private golf course when he got the idea for post-it notes. George de Mestral was on a hunting trip when he noticed burdock burs sticking to his clothes and his dog's fur. Curiosity led him to study the burs to figure out why they stuck so well. He used what he learned to create Velcro.

Ideas come to us more frequently when we are in a relaxed state of mind. The word recreation means "to create again or renew." Recreation always precedes creation. When you are fresh, you are at your best. Make sure you are investing time in your leisurely pursuits for a well-rounded life experience. Author James A. Michener said, "The master in the art of living makes little distinction between his work and his play, his labor and his leisure, his mind and his body, his information and his recreation, his love and his religion. He hardly knows which is which. He simply pursues his vision of excellence at whatever he does, leaving others to decide whether he is working or playing. To him he's always doing both." To be an effective leader, embrace work and recovery as equally important responsibilities.

GET AWAY

Howard Tinsley, PhD, an emeritus professor of psychology with Southern Illinois University, has studied the benefits of leisure since the 1970's. His immense body of research has taught us that vacationing releases two critical neurotransmitters: dopamine and serotonin. These "happy" neurotransmitters have the ability to increase focus, motivation, self-worth, enjoyment, and a host of other positive enhancers. Research revealed that workers who take more vacation time consistently receive better scores on their end-of-the-year performance reviews.

The effect isn't small, either; the boost is nearly a 10% increase! Compared to workers who didn't take time off, the vacationers also tended to be happier with their jobs and stayed with their company long-term. Americans work more hours and take less vacation than nearly 98% of other countries in the world. No wonder so many employees are stressed out and waning in their effectiveness.

If you aren't taking time to get away, let me just say, "Get out!" That's right. Get out of the office, the projects, the tasks, and go somewhere that will refresh you. And no, I am not just talking about going home or to your local hot spot; I am talking about getting away to a place with which you have no familiarity.

Each year, I have made it a habit of renting a cabin for a few nights all by myself to refresh and gain clarity from the busyness of my schedule and responsibilities. It was hard at first to leave my wife and two daughters to get away by myself, but the payoff has been incredible. I now look forward to my retreat each year because it rejuvenates me and allows me to gain new perspective.

Every few months, schedule in time to get away, even if it is just for one night. You may not feel like you need it, but don't wait to until you do, because then it will be too late. Your path to recovery and refreshment will take much longer. Regular time away keeps you feeling refreshed and ready for the next opportunity on the horizon. Just like you shouldn't wait to drink until you feel desperately thirsty, because you are already dehydrated, you also shouldn't wait to rest until you're on the brink of collapse. Be proactive about getting away from your familiar surroundings. Experience new places and new activities which will energize you. It's amazing what a small break in your schedule can do for your focus and energy.

REVIEW
5 WAYS TO GET A RAISE
#5 — LEAD YOURSELF

(5.1) Remember
      a) Perspective
      b) Hope
      c) Direction
            - Victims of Time
            - Managers of Time
            - Leaders of Time

(5.2) Resolve
      a) Prepare Yourself
      b) Position Yourself
      c) Pace Yourself

(5.3) Retreat
      a) Get Selfish
      b) Get Hobbies
      c) Get Away

Conclusion

The last thing you need to do to get a raise is to ask for one.

That's easier said than done, I know. But, if you have been practicing the steps laid out in this book, you should have more equity to negotiate a raise. The ancient statement from the Apostle James still stands true today:

"You have not, because you ask not."

It would be great if every boss automatically handed out raises, but that's not always how it works. Sometimes, you have to be your own advocate and be bold enough to ask for a raise. No one is as invested in your future as you. Make it a point each day to increase your influence, and over time, your value will grow.

Remember, timing is everything when it comes to getting a raise. You don't want to ask for a raise before you've laid a strong foundation of giving value. Influencers understand that you don't receive value until you give it. Napoleon Hill, author of Think and Grow Rich, wrote this great insight in the context of building wealth: "Instead of saying to the world, 'Show me the color of your money and I will show you what I can do,' reverse the rule and say, 'Let me show you the color of my service so that I may take a look at the color of your money if you like my service.'" He observed and studied the most highly successful people and realized one of the common denominators was the ability to give more than they received, and as a result of living this way, they received more than they could give. The mindset of highly influential people is totally different from everyone else's. Here is the difference:

- Highly Influential People: They give something before they expect to receive something.
- Everyone Else: They expect to receive something before they give something.

Never ask for a raise before you've given more than you've received. Raise your influence more and more, and you'll raise your value more and more over time. Zig Ziglar said, "When you do more than you get paid for, eventually you'll be paid for more than you do."

Great leaders are always advancing to the next level. They never stop challenging themselves to reach new heights. They know the secret to success is the capacity to lead well. In fact, true success is simply an overflow of great leadership. Yet, so many leaders and organizations feel frustratingly stuck. They are striving for success but aren't gaining any traction into growth. Their solution: work harder. But in doing so, they are just spinning their wheels in the mud.

This is where I come in. I help individuals and companies break through their limiting factors and elevate their success. A Hay Group study of Fortune 500 companies found that 21–40% utilize executive coaching; it is standard leadership development for elite executives and talented up-and-comers. An internal report of the Personnel Management Association showed that when training is combined with coaching, individuals increase their productivity by an average of 86% compared to 22% with training alone. I have been working with leaders for over 18 years. I have been personally mentored by the #1 leadership expert in the world, Dr. John C. Maxwell, to become a certified coach, speaker, and trainer on the John Maxwell Team. I have also worked with Fortune 5000 companies, entrepreneurs, non-profits, and individuals who have leveled up their success through my coaching.

I would love the opportunity to help you and/or your team develop your leadership capacity. If you would like to level up through coaching/training, here is the process to get started:

Contact Me

Let's set up a time to connect and discover what the next level is for you, your team, and your organization. We will engage with your specific leadership challenges and needs, in order to move upward together. Email: John@johnbarrettleadership.com

Customize Your Experience

My leadership coaching is designed to take you from exactly where you are to the next level. You will not find prepackaged and predetermined routines, but rather a leadership plan customized to fit your unique situation.

Coach Your Leadership

Once we have discovered your challenges and customized your plan, we will start to empower your leadership performance. This is where the magic happens as I deliver leadership coaching that will get you to the next level.

CLIMB TO NEW LEVELS

When leaders get to a whole new level, their success goes to a whole new level. Investing in your leadership development will increase your impact, influence, ideas, and income. Being coached allows you to soar to new heights.

ABOUT THE AUTHOR

John is a sought after leadership coach, speaker, and trainer. He has been living and teaching leadership for over sixteen years. John has been personally mentored by world renown leadership expert, Dr. John C. Maxwell, and a host of other highly successful leaders. He has coached Fortune 5000 companies, entrepreneurs, non-profits, and individuals who desire to level up their success.

John has been interviewed on radio programs, podcasts, blogs, and many other platforms, reaching over 200,000 listeners. He is dedicated to guiding others to the next level on their leadership journey.

www.JOHNBARRETTLEADERSHIP.com

Resources

———>>

www.ingramcontent.com/pod-product-compliance
Lightning Source LLC
Chambersburg PA
CBHW051650040426
42446CB00009B/1074